GWR
and the
General Strike
(1926)

by

C.R. Potts

THE OAKWOOD PRESS

British Library Cataloguing in Publication Data
A Record for this book is available from the British Library
ISBN 0 85361 488 1

Typeset by Oakwood Graphics.

Printed by Alpha Print (Oxford) Ltd, Witney, Oxon.

Other Oakwood Press books by the author:
The Brixham Branch (out of print)
The Newton Abbot to Kingswear Railway
Windsor to Slough: A Royal Branch Line

Published by
The Oakwood Press
P.O. Box 122, Headington, Oxford OX3 8LU

Contents

Introduction

The GWR bound its General Strike records into three very large guard books. These now form part of RAIL786 class at the Public Record Office, Kew. One volume contains the 114 pages of the superintendent of the line's (SOL) daily strike log and this very interesting document forms the basis of Chapter Two. Another valuable record included in these volumes is the departmental histories which are described in Chapter Seven. It was the finding of these volumes, back in 1988 before they went to Kew, that led me to decide to write about an event that has had next to no coverage from a railway viewpoint.

Research began in earnest in 1993 and continued, off and on, for the next three years. I decided that it would be appropriate to aim for its completion in 1996, the 70th anniversary of the Strike. After sifting through all I could find on the GWR's involvement, from records chiefly at Kew, Brunel University (the Clinker Collection), Colindale Newspaper Library and in BR's own archives, and to a lesser extent at Warwick University, it was necessary to write a chapter putting the Strike in its historical context. This entailed reading, or at least examining, many of the large number of histories published; at least twice the number listed in the Bibliography, those are the ones I found most useful. It was extremely difficult reducing the millions of words written by historians into a single summary chapter (Chapter One) and, I emphasise, I am not a trained historian. But the chapter was checked by a qualified history teacher/examiner who is himself also an author, and he did not find fault with my historical interpretation.

The other most difficult feature in the compilation of the book has been the obtaining of photographs. I have not been able to find any more contemporary pictures to include (other than some almost identical to those used, such as more scenes at Paddington stables). Bearing in mind that few papers published during the Strike and that the railways were struggling to run trains rather than record events, the dearth of photographs is not surprising. Most of those of the GWR seem to have been taken in London. I did find some unusual pictures in the *Western Morning News* (Plymouth) but unfortunately the originals were lost in the Blitz! I hope readers will not be too concerned at the lack of illustrations and that the text, most of which has never been published before, will provide its own illumination.

Having been employed for the whole of my working life (until very recently) in the railway industry, I have tried to maintain a neutral stance in the writing of this book. I have tried not to be biased either towards management or unions, although I have been critical where I felt it to be necessary. The subject is still a sensitive one, and for that reason I have rarely named names, although they are to be found in the original records.

I hope this small history will fill one of the remaining few gaps in our knowledge of the GWR in the 20th century.

February 1996

Christopher Potts
Didcot, Oxon

Chapter One

Historical Background

Before dealing with the effect of the General Strike on the GWR, it is necessary to understand the historical background which led to the General Strike. Millions of words have been written by learned historians on the reasons for the General Strike, also detailing the actions of those nine strife-torn days. But this book is a *railway* history and this chapter will set out only the facts which are essential to an understanding of the reasons for the General Strike, 70 years after the event. Subject to this, the chapter will be as concise as possible; readers who wish to study the historical background in greater depth are referred to the Bibliography. There is a great deal of material to choose from.

The roots of the General Strike - from the railwaymen's viewpoint - go back to at least the year 1919. Before this there had been only one national railway strike, a two day affair in August 1911. This had arisen because of the workers' dissatisfaction with the functioning of the Conciliation Boards set up in 1907 to deal with the men's representatives (unions were not recognised at that time) on wages and hours. Often 18 months elapsed before a grievance was dealt with by the 'Confiscation Boards', and everything possible was done to clog the works. A meeting with the Government producing nothing more than the promise of a Royal Commission to investigate the working of the conciliation agreement, and being aware that the Government would use all the civil and military force at its disposal to put down any industrial action, an immediate strike was called by the railway unions.

On receipt of the telegrams, staff walked out immediately, an estimated final total of 200,000 coming out. Within 48 hours Asquith's Liberal Government had instructed the railway companies to meet the unions' representatives and discuss the questions in dispute. With sympathetic action by some miners the effect on industry had been more serious than the Government had envisaged. The outcome was improvements to the conciliation schemes; union recognition by the management had to wait until 1917 (1919 in the case of the clerks).

In March 1912 the first ever national miners' strike started with a view to obtaining a minimum wage agreement. This continued until April and resulted in agreement for district minimum wages. It was the longest industrial conflict experienced in Britain up to that date.

In 1913 the National Union of Railwaymen (NUR) was formed out of the Amalgamated Society of Railway Servants, the United Pointsmen's and Signalmen's Society and the General Railway Workers' Union. Most of the engine drivers and firemen and railway clerks remained in independent unions.

The first quarter of the century was a period in which the decline in the value of wages was severe. If a pound is taken to have been worth a pound in 1914, by 1920 its purchasing power was only worth the equivalent of 40 pence (8 shillings), although it had slightly recovered by 1925, then being worth 56 pence (just over 11 shillings). (For interest, in 1991 its purchasing power would have been worth just two pence - less than 6*d*. in old money!)

In 1917 the Russian revolution took place and the Tsar was removed and later killed. From that time onwards, writes R. Page Arnot in his book *The General Strike Its Origins and History*, '. . . great strikes were feared not simply for their own effects, but for their latent possibilities of revolution.'

During World War I the railways had been controlled by the state, day to day control being vested in a Railway Executive Committee consisting of the General Managers of the 11 largest companies. The unions made a 'truce' agreement that all existing contracts and conditions of service would remain in operation during the war. However, because of the rapid rise in the cost of living, a series of war bonuses was agreed. These were flat rate increases, totalling eventually 33*s*. (£1.65). Because they were flat rate improvements they raised the wages of the poorest paid grades proportionately more than those of the skilled men - a porter was paid 183 per cent more in 1919 than in 1914, while a driver received only 68 per cent more. However, the 33*s*. equalled a rise of 117 per cent more on the *average* railway wage, while in the same period the cost of living had risen by between 120 and 125 per cent. So they were worse off.

> The year 1919 was one of widespread industrial and social unrest. Major industrial conflicts, looming in the summer of 1914, were postponed for the 'duration'; but no sooner had the armistice been signed than long-shelved programmes of reform were presented to employers with demands for quick satisfaction. Every day that year an average of 100,000 men were on strike.

Thus writes Philip Bagwell in his history of the NUR, *The Railwaymen*, here talking of the national, rather than railway, situation. Soon after the war, the Government conceded the 8 hour day to railwaymen, which it had agreed in principle in 1917 but had not implemented because of the national emergency. It was introduced on 1st February, 1919. In January 1919 the miners had threatened to strike and called upon the Triple Alliance (of miners, transport workers and railwaymen), put together in 1914, but never tested, to support them. However, to avoid a fight, the Government set up the Sankey Commission to look at wages and possible nationalisation of the mines. This made reports in two parts - the first in March after only 17 days proposed higher wages and shorter hours (a 7 hour day rather than 8 hours). The second part came in June, but the Committee was divided over the question of nationalisation and the Government took no action on this point, only declaring its intention of rejecting nationalisation in August 1919.

Meanwhile on the railways the companies had conceded many improvements in the wages and conditions enjoyed by drivers, firemen and cleaners but refused to extend these improvements to other grades, chiefly represented by the NUR. Standardisation of wages for these grades meant a substantial *cut* in wages because the base was made the average rate of pay for each grade, whereas drivers had been standardised on the highest rate of pay. S. Armitage in *The Politics of Decontrol of Industry* surmises that the Government wished to see the traditional differential between skilled and unskilled grades restored. An article in the *Evening News* of 1st October, 1919 said that the pay rise given to footplate staff took account of the inequality of the flat rate war bonuses paid. Although the footplatemen's union (ASLEF) had nothing to gain they decided to join with the NUR in a national strike which began on 26th September.

As was to happen later in the General Strike, the companies encouraged the use of volunteers to run the trains, whether they be civilians, retired railway 'servants' or non-striking railwaymen carrying out unusual work. At a conference with the Railway Executive Committee on 27th September the Prime Minister, Lloyd George, had pressed strongly for some sort of improvised service to be run. He said,

> . . . our experience in the war had been that work for which it had hitherto been considered five years apprenticeship was essential, could be done, after a week's training, by intelligent girls.

He said something similar again later in the Conference, expanding upon this to describe the work as that 'on which the most highly skilled engineers had been engaged could be done by women after three weeks' training.' He also expressed the view that the strike had been prompted by those who were working for a complete change in the social order (specifically exempting Mr Thomas of the NUR from this comment), and revealed that he had not signed a paper for further demobilisation (of troops) and would not do so until the Strike was over.

The Coalition Government still had control of the food supply, the wartime Ministry of Food not having been abolished. There was also an abundant supply of lorries and trained drivers, being demobilised from military use. Some 6,000 servicemen and 2,500 military lorries were used to maintain the distribution of essential supplies. For the first time there was an alternative available to distribution of goods by rail. Lloyd George wrote in the foreword to George Glasgow's book *General Strikes and Road Transport*: 'At the end of the Strike the stocks of food throughout the country were practically normal.'

An effective media campaign by the unions won over public opinion and much of the press, which had started strongly on the Government's side, after a week was admitting that the railwaymen had a good case. On 4th October a conference of other leading trades' unions sent a statement to the Prime Minister that, unless a more reasonable attitude was taken by his Cabinet, 'it would be impossible to avert a widespread extension of the Strike with all its consequences.'

That afternoon the Government capitulated. Wages would be left at the existing levels until 30th September, 1920 and would not be reduced (with the minimum set at the existing 51s., rather than the proposed 40s.) so long as the cost of living stood at not less than 110 per cent above the pre-war level.

Much more could be written here about the 1919 Strike, which in many ways was a rehearsal of what happened during the General Strike as far as the railways were concerned. The detailed reports are available, but to include them would probably double the size of this book which is, after all, about the 1926 Strike.

During the summer of 1920, in a period of rising unemployment and with the pound worth only 40 per cent of its 1914 value, the miners submitted a claim for a reduction in the price of domestic coal and an increase in wages. This was declined and, following a ballot, the miners called a strike and asked the Triple Alliance to support them. The NUR would not do so and the Transport Workers were undecided. On 16th October the miners went on strike and on 21st October the NUR had a change of mind and voted for a national railway strike in support of the miners, to start on 24th October.

This was sufficient to step up the negotiations with the miners and the NUR agreed to postpone its sympathetic strike. The miners returned to work on 3rd November, having gained a temporary wage rise and a promise of further discussions.

Following this experience the Government introduced the Emergency Powers Act, which gave the state wide powers to maintain 'essential services' during a strike and arbitrary powers over industrial disputes.

If the years since the ending of the war had been troublous, 1921 proved to be momentous for its effect on industrial relations. The slump in British industry had developed to a serious extent and the coal industry had been particularly badly affected. The coal export market had been affected by falling prices, the programme of reparations forced upon Germany after the war, and the complete loss of the Russian market. On 15th February the Government said it would end its wartime control of the mines (since 1916) and hand them back to their private owners on 31st March, 1921.

Immediately the owners said that there would have to be a return to district wage agreements and drastic wage reductions, which in the case of South Wales, for example, would mean a cut of between 40 and 50 per cent. The miners would not accept these terms and a lock-out of the coal mining industry began on 1st April, 1921. The Government invoked the Emergency Powers Act and declared a 'state of emergency.' The Triple Alliance met on 8th April and resolved to call a strike in support of the miners from 12th April, subsequently put back to 15th April, unless the Government reopened negotiations beforehand.

Speaking to a meeting of MPs in the House of Commons on 14th April, Frank Hodges, the Miners' Federation Secretary was misreported as saying that the union would consider a return to district settlements, whereas what he actually said was that only one offer had been made, and that was by the Government-entailing a return to district settlements. The Government thought they saw a loophole and asked for a meeting with the union the next day. This the miners refused. The Triple Alliance partners tried to get the miners to meet the Government and, when they refused, called off their threatened sympathetic strike. This day, Friday 15th April, was hereafter referred to in union circles as 'Black Friday' and was regarded by the miners as an act of betrayal.

The socialist historian John Murray in *The General Strike of 1926* writes as follows:

> The miners, bitter and disillusioned at the growing crisis, struggled on until June. Then they were forced back to work, their wages slashed and their agreements shattered and torn up. The great paralysis which was to grip the mining valleys through 'the

> years between' had started: the feeling of oppression and inequality which breeds despair, hate and social decay was spreading through the valleys like a cancer.
> The effects of Black Friday were enormous . . . Reductions were forced on engineers, shipyard workers, builders, seamen, cotton operators. Wages of agricultural workers were cut . . . The railways were handed back to private companies who immediately began retrenchment. By the end of 1921 wage cuts averaging 8*s*. a week had been suffered by 6 million workers.

By the middle of 1922 unemployment had reached 1½ million or 13½ per cent of the working population. In November of that year a Conservative Government (PM Bonar Law) replaced Lloyd George's Coalition Government. In May 1923 Bonar Law resigned because of ill health and was replaced by Stanley Baldwin. An election the following December was indecisive, but the Conservatives remained in power with the most seats. However, they were defeated in Parliament the following month (Jan. 1924) and were replaced by the first-ever Labour Government with Ramsay MacDonald at its head. They were, however, dependent on Liberal support. J.H. Thomas, Political General Secretary of the NUR, was appointed Colonial Secretary in MacDonald's Cabinet.

From 1st January, 1923 over 120 railway companies ranging from tiny to very large were grouped into the 'Big Four' - the GWR, SR, LMS and LNER. This was a result of the Government's involvement in running the railways during World War I. The enabling legislation was the Railways Act, 1921.

The good feeling generated towards ASLEF by the latter's support of NUR strikers in 1919 had soon dissipated and in 1924, when the roles were reversed, the NUR refused to support ASLEF in a strike of enginemen. Following pressure from traders for railway charges to be lowered, the companies had put proposals to the unions for reductions in costs. After negotiation up to National Wages Board level some of these proposals had been dropped. But the unions had reluctantly agreed to reductions in pay for Sunday duty and that mileage payments for drivers should apply after 150 miles, rather than the existing 120 miles. Although the ASLEF Executive Committee accepted this, the union's Annual Assembly of Delegates did not; a ballot of the membership decided on strike action against the mileage clauses and this began on 19th January, 1924. A comment in the *Manchester Guardian* that ASLEF was fighting the NUR quite as much as it was fighting the railway companies was accepted as accurate by the NUR leadership.

The NUR instructed its members to stay at work. The stoppage had most effect where ASLEF was strong, including much of the GWR, although in South Wales there was a strong contingent of NUR men. However, the NUR had instructed that where either the driver or fireman was an ASLEF man, a NUR replacement should not be supplied. This meant that many NUR members, although at work, sat in the cabin with nothing to do. The strike ended on 29th January, the only concessions on mileage being that the alteration in the starting point from 120 miles to 150 miles should be applied in stages over one year.

Following a temporary boom in coal exports in 1923, the miners did manage to obtain some improvements to their wage rates and conditions (including a

NOTICE TO THE STAFF.

The following is an extract from a letter dated July 30th from the National Union of Railwaymen to the Company:—

MINING CRISIS.

"With reference to the above, and the stoppage which may take place at the mines after the 31st instant, I have to inform you that in conjunction with other organisations concerned, my Executive Committee have indicated to our members who may be involved that they must not handle coal during the course of the dispute."

The Company have every desire to avoid any labour trouble, but it is necessary to remind the staff that the Great Western Railway Company are under legal obligation to convey all traffic offered to them for conveyance. It is impossible in any circumstances to countenance discrimination by the staff as to the traffic they will deal with or the circumstances in which they will handle particular traffic. It is earnestly hoped that the staff will recognise this and be loyal to the conditions of their service as railway employees.

FELIX J. C. POLE.
General Manager.

PADDINGTON STATION,
July 30*th*, 1925.

The GWR's response to the NUR's plan to aid the miners in July 1925 by placing an embargo on coal movement.

minimum wage) in 1924, but the district agreements, imposed in 1921 remained in place.

In October 1924 the Labour Government was defeated on a vote of censure and resigned. There was general disappointment with this Government amongst its supporters and a feeling that MacDonald and his colleagues had deliberately shied away from radical policies that might have been expected from Labour. This disappointment helped produce a mood in which serious industrial action became possible.

The following month a Conservative Government was elected with Baldwin as Prime Minister and Winston Churchill as Chancellor of the Exchequer.

John Murray says of the year 1925, referring to Churchill:

> . . . his inglorious decision, in the early part of 1925 [April], to return Britain to the Gold Standard*. The march to the General Strike really began at that moment. For it was the return to the Gold Standard which started the clamour for a lowering of production costs to boost exports; and a lowering of production costs meant only one thing to the industrialists of 1925 - yet another cut in wages.

An opposite view is taken of Churchill's action by biographer Martin Gilbert in *Churchill, A Life*. He says that Churchill was uneasy about the return to the Gold Standard, 'which decision he had inherited from the short-lived Labour Government.'

A combination of the expansion of German coal production, a general world recession and the return to the Gold Standard which made British exports dearer, caused the mine owners to announce on 30th June, 1925 that in a month's time they would terminate the 1924 wages agreement (with its minimum wage) and make a reduction in wages of between 13 and 48 per cent (depending on district). This said the miners, 'would transfer all the economic ills of the industry to the already over-burdened shoulders of the mineworkers, and the mine owners would assure to themselves a good profit under all conceivable circumstances . . .' and was 'too terrible to contemplate . . .' Needless to say the terms were rejected by the miners.

The TUC pledged full support to the miners (10th July); on 14th July the Government announced the setting up of a Court of Inquiry. This produced a report, condemning the owners' actions, and in favour of a fixed minimum wage. Following behind-the-scenes work between the various unions and the TUC, an Industrial Alliance (including the railway unions) was formed. On 29th July the railway unions and the T&GWU drafted plans for enforcing an embargo on coal movement. Details were published on 30th July.

Following a final meeting with the interested parties, in the early hours of Friday 31st July the Prime Minister stepped back from the brink. Announcing a nine months' subsidy to the coal industry (until 1st May, 1926), the owners would withdraw their notices and a Royal Commission of Inquiry would be set

*Gold Standard: A monetary system in which paper money was convertible on demand into gold. Banknotes were issued fractionally backed by gold (i.e. gold reserves were a fixed proportion of the value of notes in circulation). Rates of exchange between countries were fixed by their currency values in gold. Most financially important countries were on the gold standard from 1900 until its suspension in World War I because of the problems of transporting gold. It was reintroduced in 1925 but finally abandoned in 1931. [Extract from the Macmillan Encyclopaedia.]

up to study fully the workings of the industry. Only 48 hours earlier Baldwin had denied the possibility of a subsidy.

This day was afterwards referred to as 'Red Friday' in union circles.

The Government had capitulated because it realised that it was not sufficiently prepared for a full scale clash with the unions. It now began preparations in earnest, for it foresaw that a clash was inevitable and, according to John Murray, 'desirable if the trade unions, and the miners in particular, were to be brought to heel.' A semi-official organisation called the Organisation for Maintenance of Supplies (OMS) came into being, not sponsored by the Government but with its blessing. This body set about mustering volunteers prepared to maintain essential supplies and services, act as special constables etc. in the event of a General Strike. The list of names, said to be 100,000 strong, although doubts have been cast on this, was handed over to the Government just before the Strike started.

The Goverment's own arrangements were to put together a complete scheme to keep the food and transport services of the country in operation, working through 10 civil commissioners in England and Wales (Scotland was dealt with separately). These commissioners would control road transport, food and fuel supplies and be responsible for the maintenance of law and order. Commissioners had powers to requisition road transport if necessary. Secret instructions detailing the arrangements were sent out to Town Clerks in November 1925.

The unions meanwhile made no detailed preparations, but placed their faith in the Royal Commission to produce the necessary solution. It was to prove their undoing.

They did, however, attempt to revive the Industrial Alliance, in November 1925, but this was 'killed off' almost before it started by the NUR. The latter tabled a requirement that a condition of membership should be a declared intention to work towards one union for each industry. This proposal, apart from antagonising ASLEF, caused the various unions to take time-consuming ballots of their memberships, which meant that when the Strike came they had made no preparations to act as allies.

The Royal Commission, chaired by Sir Herbert Samuel, finally reported on 10th March, 1926. It was all bad news for the miners: it rejected nationalisation of the mines although it proposed nationalisation of the mineral itself (previously recommended by the Sankey Commission but ignored by the Government). The subsidy should cease on 30th April and never be repeated; the working day should be stabilised at 7½ hours (it was then 7 hours); and, finally, there must be a wage cut, said to be 'indispensable' in the interests of the industry. The miners at that time were earning between 8*s*. 5*d*. and 10s. 4*d*. a day, some 50 per cent more than in 1914, whilst the official index of the cost of living was then 75 per cent above the 1914 level. In their view the only outcome of the Inquiry was to 'provide the Government and the owners with the necessary argument for the contemplated attack on the miners' wages.' They rejected its findings on 12th March, but deferred action until after a full delegate conference to be held on 9th April.

On 8th April the TUC stated that further negotiations should take place between the parties; they were not yet ready to pledge whole-hearted support to the miners' cause. Murray says, 'The fact that a significant proportion of the Council were Freemasons did not add to their militancy . . .' Murray writes bitterly of J.H. Thomas's 'commanding' influence on the General Council:

> While the workers were squaring up for the General Strike, Thomas was cultivating friends in high society . . . Most of Thomas's biographers are agreed that he never was a Socialist . . . his aura was that of kings and princes, millionaires, dukes and ambassadors. Never workers. He used to boast of his days 'on the footplate' but dreaded the thought of having to go back, and he made sure that there was no chance of that.

The miners' conference on 9th April, as expected, resolved that the working day should not be extended, that the principle of national agreements should be adhered to and that no wage reductions should be accepted. However, at a meeting four days later the coal owners told the miners that they would abandon any national agreements they held with the Miners' Federation and would, in future, proceed only by district negotiations. The following day the TUC issued a declaration somewhat more supportive than its previous one, promising to 'render the miners the fullest support in resisting the degradation of their way of life . . .' The International Miners' Federation promised to embargo the movement of coal to replace British supplies.

Events now moved to the inevitable conclusion. The Prime Minister presided over a meeting between the coal owners and the miners on 22nd April which broke up in deadlock. The owners refused to discuss a minimum wage based on a national agreement. Approaches afterwards to the Prime Minister by the TUC proved fruitless. Baldwin said that the owners would not even accept the Samuel Report unless the miners first agreed to accept a 13 per cent wage cut.

In the last week the meetings came thick and fast. On 26th and 27th April Mr Baldwin met the TUC and asked them to supply some representatives to sit with the miners on the negotiating council to meet the coal owners, but the latter turned down this suggestion. On 27th April the TUC, at last, began preparing for the now inevitable strike - far too late, of course. On 28th April the miners called a special delegate conference and on 29th April the TUC summoned an emergency conference of all affiliated Union Executives. This continued for 2½ days, finishing in the afternoon of Saturday 1st May, although adjourned during Friday 30th April to enable the TUC and the miners to meet the Prime Minister. After 12 long hours of discussion, this meeting ended in stalemate. A last minute proposal by the coal owners to reinstate a national minimum wage (involving a wage reduction of 13 per cent) based on an *eight* hour day for at least three years, then to be reviewed, was turned down by the miners. As they pointed out, their present hours were long enough to supply all the coal for which a market could be found, and extended hours would simply swell the dole queues.

When the adjourned conference resumed at midday on Saturday 1st May, a vote was taken on a co-ordinated strike policy proposed by the TUC. The trades to stop work were: transport, printing, iron & steel, metal, heavy chemicals, engineering and building (except housing and hospitals). The unions supplying gas and electricity power were urged to co-operate 'with the object of ceasing to supply power', but no restrictions would be permitted as far as health, food and sanitary services were concerned. The miners were already locked-out, the coal owners having ended existing contracts on 30th April. The vote in favour of striking was 3,653,527 and 49,911 against. From the platform Ernest Bevin revealed, after the result of the vote was announced, that the TUC had only prepared its Strike memorandum the previous night when it discovered that the Government had signed an order for the use of the Emergency Powers Act, and had begun printing recruiting posters for volunteers.

Despite its complete lack of preparation, and the opposition of such people as J.H. Thomas and Ramsay MacDonald, the leader of the Labour party, the die had been cast, and the TUC announced that the chosen trades should cease work from midnight on Monday 3rd May, 1926.

Emergency Powers Act, 1920.

Extract from Emergency Regulations, dated April 30th, 1926.

20. (1) If any person injures, or does any act calculated to injure, or to prevent the proper use or working of, any public building, railway, canal, bridge, road, tramway, vehicle, telegraph or telephone line, cable or plant, mine, shop, factory, waterworks, gasworks, electric generating station, or any works or plant used or adapted for use for the production, supply, storage, or transport of food, fuel, munitions, water, light, heat, or power, he shall be guilty of an offence against these regulations.

(2) If any person approaches or is in the neighbourhood of or enters any such place as aforesaid with intent to do injury thereto he shall be guilty of an offence against these regulations: and notwithstanding that no such act or injury is committed by him, he shall be deemed to be guilty of such an offence if by reason of his being in possession of any explosive or incendiary substance or lethal weapon or dangerous missile, or otherwise from the circumstances of the case or his conduct or his known character as proved, it appears that his purpose was to do such injury.

21. (1) If any person attempts or does any act calculated or likely to cause mutiny, sedition or disaffection among any of His Majesty's forces, or among the members of any police force, or any fire brigade, or among the civilian population, or to impede, delay or restrict any measures taken for securing and regulating the supply or distribution of food, water, fuel, light or other necessities, or for maintaining the means of transit or of locomotion, or for any other purposes essential to the public safety or the life of the community, he shall be guilty of an offence against these regulations.

Provided that a person shall not be guilty of an offence under this regulation by reason only of his taking part in a strike or peacefully persuading any other person to take part in a strike.

* * * * * *

32 (1) If any person contravenes or otherwise fails to comply with any of the provisions of these regulations or any order or direction made or given thereunder, or is guilty of an offence against these regulations, he shall be liable on summary conviction to imprisonment with or without hard labour for a term not exceeding three months, or to a fine not exceeding one hundred pounds, or to both such imprisonment and fine, and shall be liable to forfeit to the Crown any goods or money in respect of which the offence was committed.

* * * * * *

An extract from the Emergency Powers Act, 1920, which the Government implemented on 30th April, 1926.

Sir Felix Pole, the General Manager of the GWR at the time of the General Strike. He had joined the company as a junior telegraph clerk in October 1891 at the age of 14, becoming General Manager in 1921, aged only 44, and left the company in July 1929 to become Chairman of AEI Ltd. Perhaps surprisingly, and to Sir Felix's regret, the Directors of the GWR never asked him to become a Director after he had left the company. *British Rail*

R.H. Nicholls was superintendent of the line at the time of the General Strike. He had joined the GWR in 1884 as a clerk in the SOL office, later transferring to the London division 'where he filled practically every position at stations and in the divisional office', becoming chief clerk to the divisional superintendent in 1904 and assistant divisional superintendent in 1907. In 1911 he went back to the SOL's office as an assistant and worked his way up to the top job by 1919. He remained in that exalted position until his retirement on 31st December, 1932. He was a very popular Great Western officer (although perhaps not in 1926!). *Railway Gazette*

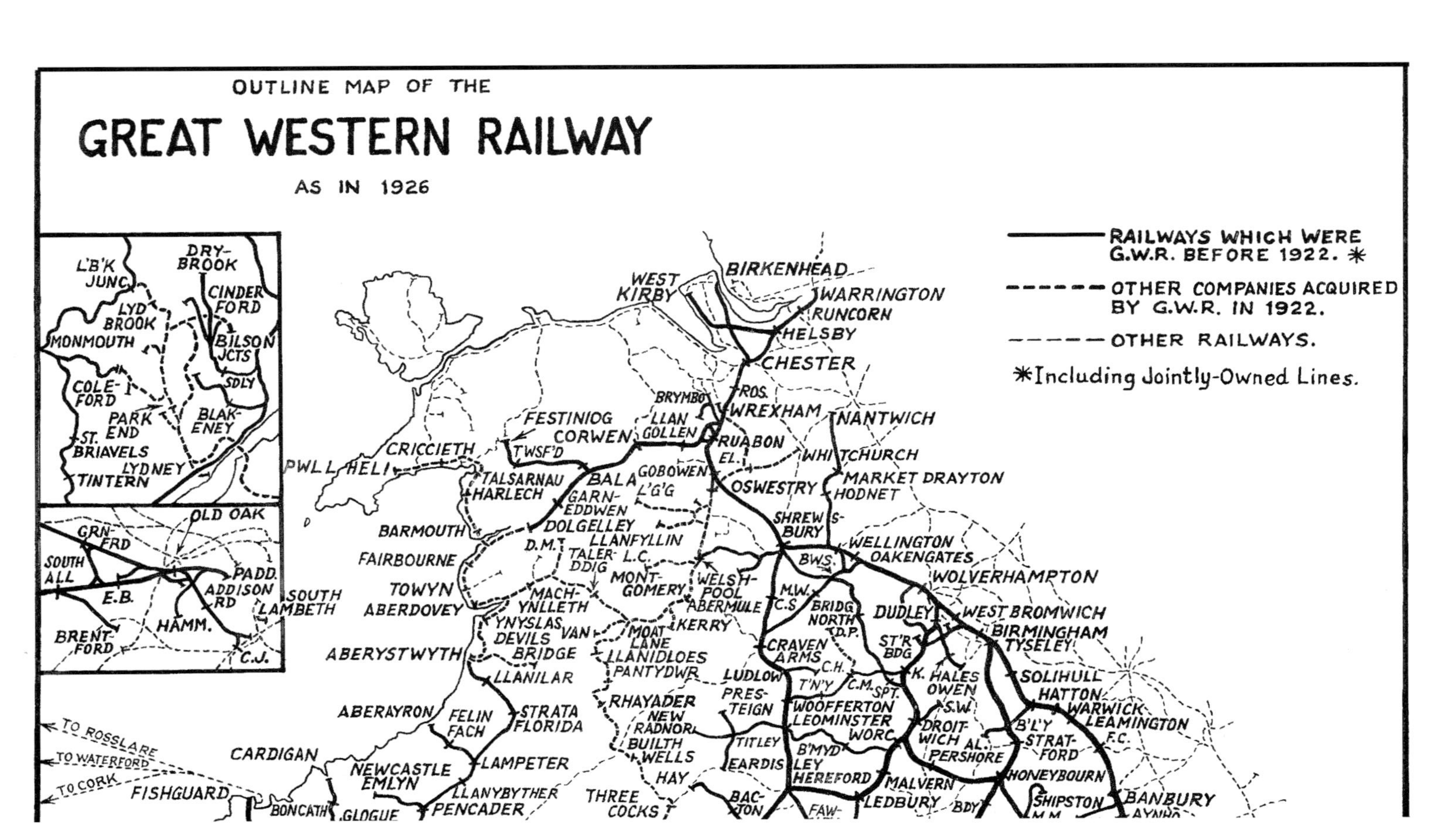

OUTLINE MAP OF THE
GREAT WESTERN RAILWAY
AS IN 1926
RAILWAYS WHICH WERE G.W.R. BEFORE 1922. *
OTHER COMPANIES ACQUIRED BY G.W.R. IN 1922.
OTHER RAILWAYS.
*Including Jointly-Owned Lines.
L'B'K JUNC.
DRY-BROOK
CINDER FORD
LYD BROOK
MONMOUTH
BILSON JCTS
SDLY
COLE-FORD
PARK END
BLAK-ENEY
ST. BRIAVELS
LYDNEY
TINTERN
OLD OAK
GRN-FRD
SOUTH ALL
PADD.
ADDISON RD
E.B.
HAMM.
BRENT-FORD
C.J.
SOUTH LAMBETH
WEST KIRBY
BIRKENHEAD
WARRINGTON
RUNCORN
HELSBY
CHESTER
ROS.
BRYMBO
WREXHAM
NANTWICH
FESTINIOG
LLAN GOLLEN
CORWEN
RUABON
EL.
WHITCHURCH
MARKET DRAYTON
HODNET
CRICCIETH
TWSF'D
PWLLHELI
TALSARNAU
HARLECH
BALA
GOBOWEN
L'G'G
OSWESTRY
GARN-EDDWEN
DOLGELLEY
SHREWSBURY
BARMOUTH
D.M.T.
LLANFYLLIN
TALER-DDIG
L.C.
WELLINGTON
OAKENGATES
FAIRBOURNE
BWS.
WOLVERHAMPTON
TOWYN
MONT-GOMERY
WELSH-POOL
MACH-YNLLETH
M.W. C.S.
ABERMULE
ABERDOVEY
BRIDG NORTH
D.P.
DUDLEY
WEST BROMWICH
YNYSLAS
VAN
MOAT LANE
KERRY
BIRMINGHAM
TYSELEY
DEVILS BRIDGE
CRAVEN ARMS
ST'R BDG
ABERYSTWYTH
LLANIDLOES
PANTYDWR
C.H.
LUDLOW
K.
HALES OWEN
SOLIHULL
LLANILAR
T'N'Y
C.M. SPT.
HATTON
RHAYADER
PRES-TEIGN
WOOFFERTON
LEOMINSTER
S.W.
WARWICK
LEAMINGTON
ABERAYRON
FELIN FACH
STRATA FLORIDA
NEW RADNOR
WORC.
DROIT-WICH
B'L'Y
STRAT-FORD
F.C.
BUILTH WELLS
TITLEY
B'MYD LEY
AL. PERSHORE
CARDIGAN
NEWCASTLE EMLYN
LAMPETER
EARDIS LEY
HEREFORD
MALVERN
HONEYBOURN
TO ROSSLARE
TO WATERFORD
TO CORK
HAY
FISHGUARD
LLANYBYTHER
THREE COCKS
BAC-TON
LEDBURY
BDY
SHIPSTON
BANBURY
BONCATH
GLOGUE
PENCADER
FAW-

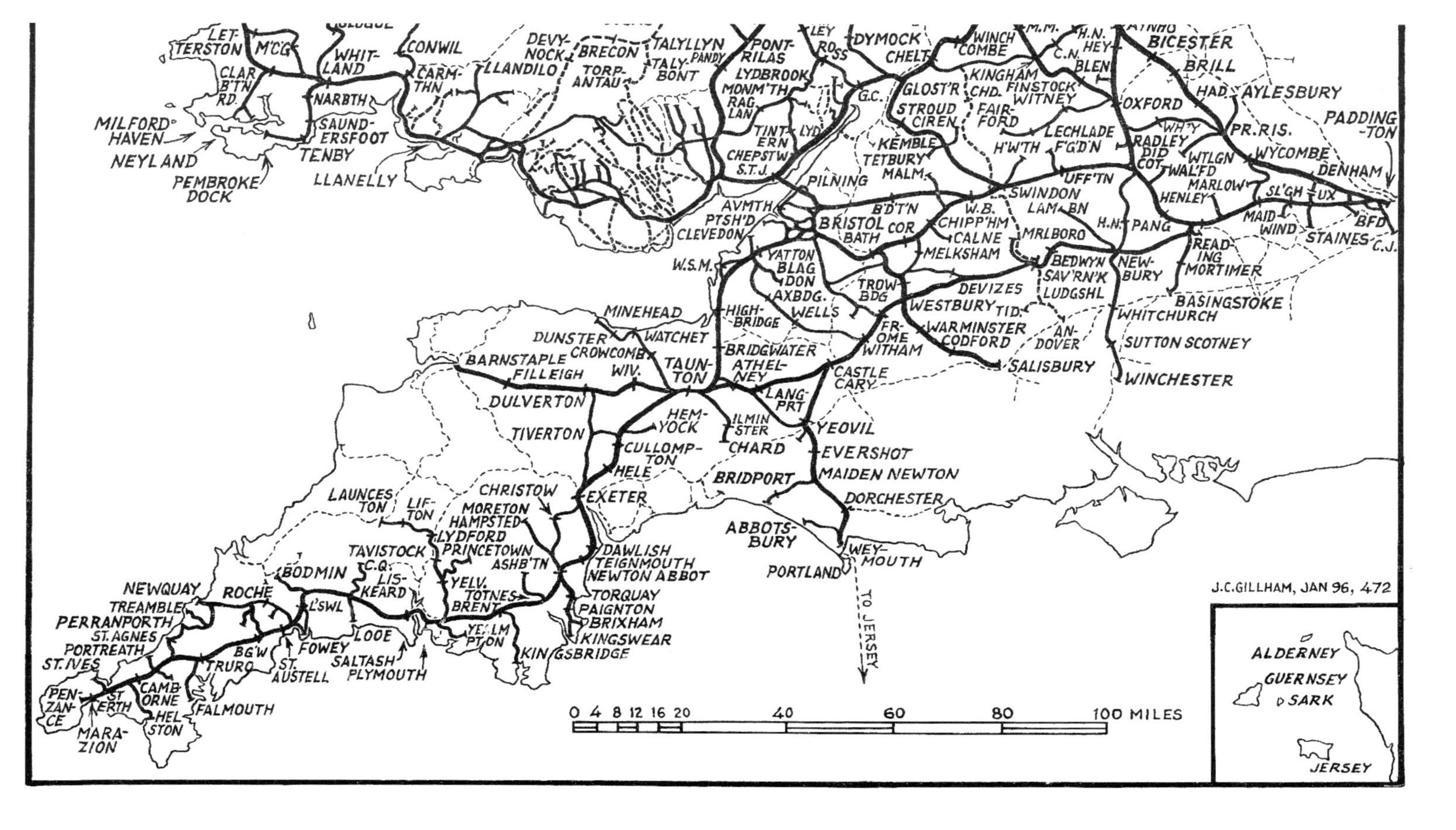

LET-TERSTON
M'C'G
CLAR B'T'N RD.
WHIT-LAND
NARBTH
SAUND-ERSFOOT
TENBY
MILFORD HAVEN
NEYLAND
PEMBROKE DOCK
CONWIL
CARM-THN
LLANELLY
LLANDILO
DEVY-NOCK
BRECON
TORP-ANTAU
TALYLLYN
TALY-BONT
PANDY
PONT-RILAS
LYDBROOK
MONM'TH
RAG. LAN
TINT-ERN
CHEPSTW
S.T.J.
LYD
ROSS
DYMOCK
CHELT
G.C.
GLOST'R
STROUD
CIREN
KEMBLE
TETBURY
MALM.
PILNING
WINCH COMBE
KINGHAM
CHD.
FINSTOCK
WITNEY
FAIR-FORD
LECHLADE
H'W'TH
F'G'D'N
UFF'TN
SWINDON
H.N.
HEY
C.N.
BLEN
OXFORD
BICESTER
BRILL
HAD.
AYLESBURY
WH'Y
RADLEY
DID COT
WTLGN
WAL'FD
PR.RIS.
WYCOMBE
PADDING-TON
DENHAM
MARLOW
HENLEY
SL'GH
UX
BFD
MAID.
WIND
STAINES
C.J.
AVMTH
PTSH'D
CLEVEDON
B'D'T'N
BRISTOL
BATH
COR
W.B.
CHIPP'HM
CALNE
MELKSHAM
LAM. BN
MRLBORO
H.N.
PANG
READ-ING
MORTIMER
W.S.M.
YATTON
BLAG DON
AXBDG.
WELLS
TROW-BDG
DEVIZES
BEDWYN
SAV'RN'K
LUDGSHL
NEW-BURY
BASINGSTOKE
WESTBURY
TID.
WHITCHURCH
MINEHEAD
HIGH-BRIDGE
FR-OME
WITHAM
WARMINSTER
CODFORD
AN-DOVER
SUTTON SCOTNEY
DUNSTER
WATCHET
CROWCOMB
BRIDGWATER
SALISBURY
BARNSTAPLE
FILLEIGH
WIV.
TAUN-TON
ATHEL-NEY
CASTLE CARY
WINCHESTER
DULVERTON
LANG-PRT
HEM-YOCK
ILMIN STER
YEOVIL
TIVERTON
CULLOMP-TON
CHARD
EVERSHOT
HELE
BRIDPORT
MAIDEN NEWTON
LAUNCES TON
LIF-TON
CHRISTOW
EXETER
DORCHESTER
MORETON HAMPSTED
ABBOTS-BURY
LYDFORD
WEY-MOUTH
TAVISTOCK
PRINCETOWN
DAWLISH
TEIGNMOUTH
NEWTON ABBOT
ASHB'TN
PORTLAND
BODMIN
C.Q.
LIS-KEARD
YELV.
TOTNES
TORQUAY
NEWQUAY
ROCHE
BRENT
PAIGNTON
TREAMBLE
L'SWL
YEALM PT'ON
BRIXHAM
PERRANPORTH
LOOE
KINGSWEAR
ST. AGNES
BG'W
FOWEY
PORTREATH
SALTASH
KINGSBRIDGE
ST. IVES
TRURO
ST. AUSTELL
PLYMOUTH
TO JERSEY
PEN-ZAN-CE
ST ERTH
CAMB-ORNE
FALMOUTH
HEL STON
MARA-ZION
0 4 8 12 16 20 40 60 80 100 MILES
J.C.GILLHAM, JAN 96, 472
ALDERNEY
GUERNSEY
SARK
JERSEY

GREAT WESTERN RAILWAY.

NOTICE TO THE STAFF.

The National Union of Railwaymen have intimated that railwaymen have been asked to strike without notice to-morrow night. Each Great Western man has to decide his course of action, but I appeal to all of you to hesitate before you break your contracts of service with the old Company, before you inflict grave injury upon the Railway Industry, and before you arouse ill feeling in the Railway service which will take years to remove.

Railway Companies and Railwaymen have demonstrated that they can settle their disputes by direct negotiations. The Mining Industry should be advised to do the same.

Remember that your means of living and your personal interests are involved, and that Great Western men are trusted to be loyal to their conditions of service in the same manner as they expect the Company to carry out their obligations and agreements.

FELIX J. C. POLE.
General Manager.

PADDINGTON STATION,
May 2nd. 1926.

7765-5-26

Your company needs you! The General Manager's plea not to 'break your contracts with the old Company'.

Chapter Two

As it Happened: The Superintendent of the Line's Daily Log*

Friday 30th April to Midnight Monday 3rd May

Most of Friday was spent 'testing the water' over the length and breadth of the GWR. In the afternoon the Chairman of United Dairies was assured that the running of milk trains would receive the company's 'first consideration'. At 4.50 pm the divisional superintendents were told to keep their offices open throughout the night. Just after 5.00 pm the miners turned down the government's latest offer and soon after that the GWR was advised that two trains of naval ratings, 600 men, plus horses and vehicles would be required from Devonport to Bury, Lancs at short notice. Soon afterwards a further train was ordered from Plymouth to Paddington, or Waterloo, with 248 men.

At 11.28 pm the General Manager's office reported that negotiations with the miners had broken down and that the miners would definitely strike. This news was telephoned to Sir Felix Pole at home in Calcot (Reading), Mr Nicholls SOL (in the GWR Hotel) and all the divisional superintendents.

During Saturday morning, 1st May the GWR imposed a 'stop' on acceptance of empty coal wagons for South Wales, and the SR, LMS and LNER imposed similar restrictions on empties for collieries in their areas. At this stage there had not been any indication that railwaymen would strike and at 12.45 pm all superintendents were wired that normal services would operate next week, but to expect a 10-15 per cent reduction the following week.

During the afternoon information started to circulate that the TUC had decided that there would be a strike in the 'vital services' if no settlement was reached in the meantime. Workers in these services would cease work on Monday night. However talks with the Government continued, a meeting with the Prime Minister at 8.30 pm adjourning at 1.30 am on Sunday morning, 2nd May.

Just after 6 on Sunday morning, Swansea Control complained that three or four large batches of empties had been received from the Cardiff and Newport divisions during the night despite the 'stop', and the SOL office had to remind those divisions to adhere to instructions. At lunchtime Mr Nicholls sent the following personal telegram to all superintendents:

> Labour situation. Want you to strain every nerve to see that milk traffic is dealt with. Rely upon you making very special efforts in this direction. Give personal attention.

At 1.00 pm Sir Felix Pole's plea to the men not to strike, containing his now-famous reference to 'the old company' was telephoned to the superintendents (*see illustration*), with instructions that it be circularised to each station, and as many local newspapers as possible.

Talks between the TUC and the Prime Minister were resumed at 2.45 pm. In

* This material can be found in RAIL786 at PRO, Kew.

Exeter St David's looking west from the up main/up relief island platform, probably in the 1930s (gas lighting survived until 1946). The three main line signal boxes here East, Middle, behind the photographer) and West (beyond the platform ends in the distance) were being worked by two signalling inspectors on 4th May. East and Middle boxes were 374 yards apart, while West box was 506 yards beyond Middle, so volunteers must have taken over before long! There was some problem with reinstatement at Exeter after the Strike, *see Chapter 8*.

L. Waters Collection

Would-be passengers consult the emergency timetable blackboards at Paddington's No. 1 platform.

GWR Magazine

the early evening messages started to circulate that the NUR and the Railway Clerks' Association (RCA) had called their members out at midnight Monday night (or 'on completion of Monday's duty' in the case of the RCA).

A telephone poll of the divisional superintendents at 12.15 am on Monday 3rd May did not reveal much in the way of definite information, but men at Worcester and in the Newport division were ready to strike.

At 12.45 am the Central News Agency stated that the talks had just broken up, it was feared in failure, and that the *Daily Mail* would not be printed because some of the printing staff had objected to the leading article. However, the first part of this statement was later corrected as the earlier talks had involved the Cabinet, but they were, in fact, continuing with the Prime Minister. At 2.30 am Central News reported that talks had completely broken down, and that the Government had called for 'immediate and unconditional withdrawal of the instructions for a General Strike' before talks could resume. An hour later the TUC expressed regret that the Government had broken off negotiations 'which appeared to give promise of leading to a settlement'.

Most of Monday was spent in obtaining information from the divisional superintendents as to the reaction of the men at the various stations and depots. A special with 6 officers and 253 naval ratings was ordered for 11.00 am from Plymouth to Paddington (actual departure was 12 noon). In the afternoon Birmingham passed on a request from the Leamington crew of the 5.15 pm goods Bordesley to Old Oak Common, who were 'double home' (lodged overnight in London), that they be allowed to change over at Bicester, as happened on Saturdays, but the request was declined.

At 7.15 pm on Monday evening the superintendents were told to set up centres for the registration of volunteers (in accordance with an instruction of 22nd October, 1920). Arrangements were made for the 5.10 pm fish train from Milford Haven to Paddington to run four hours earlier than normal and 'although delivery in London cannot be guaranteed, the best shall be done'.

At 10.50 pm Plymouth phoned to say that staff who wished not to strike were being warned by NUR members that *they* would not return to work until the loyal staff were dismissed. The SOL said that such statements should be ignored 'and that the company would stand by the loyalists'.

So the minutes ticked inexorably by and the hands of Messrs Kay's clocks all over the GWR clicked their way closer and closer to midnight. At 11.35 pm the Press Association stated that the strike would start at midnight, and just 10 minutes before midnight the Ministry of Labour confirmed that statement.

The General Strike was on!

Tuesday 4th May

The very first strike action recorded in the SOL office log happened only 15 minutes into the strike. The enginemen of the 11.00 pm goods from Southall to Paddington stabled their train and took the engine to shed. Just 5 minutes later, at 12.20 am, the huge Paddington Goods station shut down. The last train to leave there was the 11.35 pm departure (at 11.48 pm). Both shunting engines at

Old Oak Common returned to shed.

Now the Strike had started, the telephone calls to the SOL office came through thick and fast. Many divisions reported that staff, booking on before midnight for the night turn of duty, saw their shift out before joining the Strike, but this was by no means universal, and there were many reports of staff leaving duty immediately. A large number of Bristol staff, including some signalmen, struck, whereas the Exeter and Plymouth divisions reported that the night men worked normally. The London division was 'practically "dead" all points'. In the Newport and Cardiff divisions no men signed on after midnight; in Birmingham most of the night staff did not sign on, and some enginemen on duty before midnight returned to shed.

At 2.30 am Reading advised that the Oxford signalmen had walked out, and that the district inspector was on his way from Didcot to reopen the boxes, it was hoped with the aid of the platform inspector. At Bristol, inspectors were manning East, West, South Wales Junction and Dr Day's signal boxes. In the outlying boxes, the majority of the night signalmen remained on duty until 6 am.

An early attempt (2.35 am) to obtain volunteers to move milk traffic from Paddington station met with no success, despite contact with several Government officials. At 4.10 am Mr Wainwright (Cardiff division) advised that practically the whole of his staff, except the signalmen, were out on strike. He did not anticipate that any staff would be on duty after 6 am.

By now Paddington station was practically full of overnight (up) trains, 11 of which had arrived between 12.20 and 3.52 am. Only platforms 1, 2 and 5 were empty and the station was full of milk traffic. A request had been made of the Ministry of Transport and the Cabinet Secretary for between 50 and 100 volunteers to move it, but so far without success. At 5.08 am the Neyland 'perishables' arrived in platform 2 and at 5.55 am the 6.45 pm mail ex-Penzance arrived in platform 1, just 5 minutes before the Arrival and Departure boxes closed, with no-one available to man them.

The divisional superintendents now began to ring in with a progress report of the early turn. Plymouth reported 10 main line signal boxes still open, including North Road West; 10 signalmen in the Worcester division reported at 6 am. On the other hand, Newport, Swansea, London, Exeter, Gloucester and Birmingham reported low attendance; in the latter division the Tyseley station master was on strike.

Great efforts were made that morning to run a milk train from Swindon at 9.35 am to Paddington and a passenger train also ran from Bristol to Paddington. This was manned by a Yatton driver with limited road knowledge 'but ticket collector will take charge who knows road well'. The 7.10 am from Oxford ran, arriving in the last unoccupied Paddington platform (No. 5) at 10.40 am.

Gloucester advised that a train conveying milk had left that place at 11.05 am for Cardiff manned by a Bullo Pill driver and Newport guard. In the afternoon Worcester reported that they had four engines in steam, but no-one to man them. Bristol stated that out of a normal staff of roughly 500 sets of enginemen, not one man was available. They also had a large number of milk churns on hand at various stations but no prospect of moving them.

Exeter reported at lunchtime that he had one driver on duty at Exeter and none at Taunton. There was one signalman at Exeter East and one at Teignmouth (both due to close at 2 pm). The district inspectors at Taunton and Newton Abbot were each working two boxes (with the aid of bicycles one hopes!), while the chief inspector and district inspector at Exeter were employed in the Exeter boxes.

At about 2 pm the SOL sent a message to all superintendents that for the next few days work should only take place in daylight hours ('this has obvious advantages, including opportunity for working staff to take rest'). He also asked for special attention to working of level crossings (by volunteers).

At 3.20 pm Bristol reported that the Steventon station master and all his staff had gone off duty, leaving the level crossing gates across the line (this was the 'normal' position). Later that afternoon a clerk from Bristol DSO was sent to Steventon to work the level crossing, until a volunteer could be found. On arrival he found that the Wantage Rd SM had managed to staff the crossings.

At 4 pm the SOL suggested to his superintendents that more could be done to man engines, and he hoped that they were in close contact with the locomotive superintendents. Bristol replied almost immediately that he could supply two engines tomorrow, one with a Yatton driver, the other with a retired Bristol driver. This set more enquiries in motion as to whether more could be done using retired drivers. In the meantime some 50 or 60 loyal clerks and 50 students from University College were sent to Royal Oak signalling school, and each group given 1½ hours of instruction in signalling. Further sessions were to be given the following day.

At 5.20 pm an offer was made by the Strike Committee at Penzance to run a train conveying 80 tons of fish to London, on condition that no passengers were conveyed but a coach was attached to carry railwaymen stranded at Penzance. The company would not accept these terms.

Despite pressure locally by the Food Committee, the Bristol division was unable to move perishable traffic as all the enginemen were on strike. The superintendent also reported that the Corsham station master had walked out, but that he had sent a clerk from Bristol to take charge.

The company provided buses and lorries that evening to take the working staff at Paddington offices home to variously, Windsor, Slough, Uxbridge, Southall and Ealing. A similar provision was made to bring them back the next morning. At 6.30 pm a semi-fast train left for Bristol, followed at 6.40 pm by a fast train for the same place.

Chester had managed to run several trains as follows: Chester-Bala; Chester-Ruabon and back; Bala-Ruabon; Ruabon-Barmouth; Barmouth-Bala; Shrewsbury-Welshpool and back (LMS men); Shrewsbury-Hereford and back (LMS men); Chester-Manchester (LMS men) and Chester-Birkenhead and back. He had one driver at Bala and one at Chester, and reported that pickets were 'interfering' with the men coming on duty.

At 9.20 pm a message from Sir Felix Pole was sent to all divisions to the effect that clerks out on strike were not to be taken back unless there was essential work to do, or they were prepared to accept work elsewhere (not necessarily clerical).

The station master at Tyseley was probably the second most important person in that grade on the GWR to go on strike (after Caerphilly). He was in class 3 and had a staff of 33 including 3 booking clerks, 6 signalmen and 9 passenger guards. In 1926 paybill costs were £5,272 and receipts £9,490, but the latter seem to have been severely affected by the Strike having been £11,282 in 1925. *Lens of Sutton*

One of the most militant areas in GWR territory during the Strike appears to have been Llanelly, but this is not surprising when it is remembered that in August 1911, during the first ever national railway strike, soldiers had been ordered to intervene when a crowd of strikers had stopped a train there. The Riot Act was read but the strikers would not move and advanced towards the soldiers, despite shots being fired over their heads. The soldiers then opened fire on the crowd and two strikers were killed and several others injured. This picture of the by then 'Llanelli' was taken on 28th October, 1972 looking west with one of the troublesome level crossings in the distance. *J.C. Gillham*

A 5.15 pm passenger train from Cardiff arrived at Paddington at 10.37 pm.

A small amount of milk had been arriving at Paddington throughout the day, but at 10.10 pm advice was received that a milk train had left Westbury for Paddington with 607 churns on board, also two coaches conveying passengers from the Channel Islands boat. This service arrived at Paddington at 1.30 am (Wednesday).

Wednesday 5th May

The main excitement of this day was the movement of some 118 tons of fish from Milford Haven to Paddington, and it will be better to deal with this little story in one piece, rather than breaking it up as it appears in the SOL log, reported amongst other events throughout the day.

The saga started at 6.40 am with advice that the Swansea locomotive superintendent was motoring to Milford to try and arrange the manning of an engine. At 10.20 am, Mr Lea, the divisional superintendent, phoned to say that his district inspector had said that the train would not be allowed to run through Llanelly: 'There is intense feeling in the town and the district inspector says that anybody who works Llanelly box will incur grave risk'. The local police were in agreement with this assessment. The locomotive inspector and foreman (at Milford Haven?) had refused to work the train, and efforts were being made to persuade the Neyland foreman to assist.

At 11 am Swansea again phoned to report that all the clerks in the Llanelly area had walked out, following pressure from other unions. The chief booking clerk and his deputy did not want to strike, but were afraid to stay on duty. The divisional chief inspector was saying that the fish train would not get through Llanelly in any circumstances.

Two hours later Swansea superintendent spoke to Mr Nicholls personally. The footplate staff would be two firemen, one from Whitland and one from Neyland - no driver or supervisor could be provided. He was very reluctant to run the train in view of the situation at Llanelly. However, Mr Nicholls said that the local police had been alerted to the situation, and that further instructions would follow.

During the afternoon the GWR chief of police received two telegrams, one from the (civil) police superintendent at Llanelly ('cannot ensure through passage of train - refer matter to chief constable') and the other from the chief constable of Carmarthenshire hinting that he would prefer that the train did not run, but if it did to be given as much notice as possible. At 5.20 pm the SOL office spoke to the civil commissioner for South Wales, the Earl of Clarendon, explaining the background and asked that he would support the company's efforts to run the train. The Earl agreed with this course, and said he would take the necessary steps with the police to arrange protection.

Armed with this information, Mr Nicholls spoke personally to Mr Lea at 5.45 pm. He told him to start the train at once and to arrange for the boxes at Llanelly to be manned. Mr Lea replied that the Whitland district inspector, Mr Williams, would do this and that the train would start about 6.15 pm; it actually left at 6.30 pm with 15 vans on.

At 8.26 pm the SOL log reports the bald statement: 'Milford fish train passed Llanelly at 8.10 pm'. Not until 2.10 am Thursday did the full story come out. The train had run through the gates at Old Castle Crossing but those at Llanelly station had been worked by Inspector Williams. A large crowd had assembled and there had been considerable booing, but no actual violence. The trainmen had been 'interviewed' by the strikers, but as Mr Lea and Mr H. Williams had joined the train and travelled with it to Cardiff, this doubtless prevented any violence.

There is a nice tailpiece to the story. At 11.30 am on Thursday Mr Lea telephoned to say that the Food Controller at Cardiff was asking why the fish had been sent to London 'where there is understood to be plenty of fish' when it could have been disposed of in South Wales. The Cabinet were apparently interested in the matter, he suggested, and would probably ask Sir Felix Pole for information. (One sees the shadow of Sir Felix Pole over Mr Nicholls and his staff, governing their actions throughout this particular incident, and probably many others.) On Friday, however, the Chief Commissioner confirmed the correctness of the GWR's actions; doubtless some 'behind the scenes' work had taken place to ensure this.

Mr Lea said that his district inspectors would not work the Llanelly boxes, and it was very unlikely that a repeat performance of running the Milford fish could be arranged. He also asked that the Chief Engineer be asked to make arrangements to patrol the lines in his division, as was being done elsewhere.

Turning to the other events on this second day of the Strike, at noon the superintendents were advised that men, other than supervisory staff, who asked to return to work might do so, provided their services were required. A down special goods from Southall had been intended to call at Cholsey to pick up perishable traffic, but the station master refused to open the box. The London divisional superintendent arranged to send someone to Cholsey (with the train?) to open the box.

Advice from Bristol after lunch stated that Mr MacDermot (later of 'GWR History' fame) was working South Wales Junction box, and a retired chief inspector, Bristol West. Other boxes were manned by clerks; at Weston-super-Mare the station master was working both boxes, *and* attending to station duties! Mid-afternoon Gloucester advised that the Cirencester and Tetbury branches would be open tomorrow.

At the London end of the GWR, the divisional superintendent reported that large, hostile crowds were lining the canal bank at Old Oak Common and intimidating the volunteer signalmen. Mr Nicholls spoke to the GWR chief of police personally, and asked him to arrange additional protection.

At 6 pm Birmingham telephoned with some good news: 148 volunteers had been registered that day; in addition a 5 pm special had left for Paddington with 7 coaches and 'a good load of passengers' (actually 53 it later transpired).

At 9.45 pm London divisional office telephoned to say that there were seven West of England and three South Wales passenger guards stranded in London, prepared to work trains but only in the direction of their homes. London asked whether, as no trains were in mind for them to work, they could be returned as passengers *'instead of keeping them here on expenses'*. The official on duty in the SOL office told the division the men were not to return as passengers, but should be utilised to work suitable trains as required. Against this entry in the log an unknown hand, but possibly that of Sir Felix Pole as the log is bound in a volume from the General Manager's office, has written: 'No - if these men won't do work required they can't have expenses'. The SOL was duly advised of this edict.

The Ministry of Transport phoned at 10.15 pm to say that Birmingham was running out of petrol, and asked that the company do all possible to move a train of tanks, standing at Portishead, to the second city. An eventful day was rounded off by a call from Birmingham at midnight to report, *inter alia*, that the signalman at Soho, freshly returned from special leave, had reported for duty at his own box - he was an NUR representative!

Thursday 6th May

Events took a more serious turn with information received that about 50 keys had been removed from their chairs in the permanent way, about 100 yds from the Treforest end of Pontypridd tunnel.

The early morning summary of staff reporting for duty included advice that 2,900 cans of milk had arrived at Paddington in the 24 hrs up to 9 pm Wednesday. Mid-morning, Birmingham telephoned to say that the Earl of Dudley, and some other owners of private locomotives, had put six or eight qualified shunting engine drivers at the company's disposal.

At 12.50 pm London division reported problems at West Ealing and Hayes, where track circuits had failed owing to the batteries running down. The volunteer signalmen were unable to lower the protecting signals and they were having to be passed at danger. Mr Insell, the signal engineer, was asked to arrange for the track circuits to be disconnected.

The LNER Control at Liverpool Street reported a service of four trains each way between Marylebone and High Wycombe for the first time. Trains would leave London at 10.30 am, 12.55, 2.10 and 6.0 pm and return from High Wycombe at 12.40, 3.0, 4.0, and 7.45 pm. Later, information was given that actually five trains ran each way.

The Windsor branch reopened this day, the first train leaving Slough for Windsor at 3.48 pm. The Staines branch also reopened, with connections at West Drayton off the 5.0, 5.15 and 5.45 pm trains from Paddington. One trip was also run from Maidenhead to High Wycombe, and it was hoped to open the branch the following day.

A call from Birmingham at 6 pm gave news of incidents of stone throwing at the signalman at Victoria Basin, and at the driver of the 3.35 pm Wolverhampton to Shrewsbury between Wolverhampton and Dunstall Park. The police had been called in.

Efforts were initiated to run five banana specials from the Bristol area the next day, although Bristol superintendent complained that engines and men working from Bristol were not being returned to him, and he could not run the banana trains unless they were.

The last two messages of a less eventful day than the one before concerned advice from the Underground that they intended to reopen the Ealing-Wood Lane service tomorrow; and a call from Plymouth that five liners would disembark some 550 passengers at Millbay Docks and it was intended to run a special service from North Road to Paddington at about 1 pm on Friday.

Friday 7th May

Between 10 pm Thursday and 4 am, no less than 2,521 churns of milk were received at Paddington. In the morning the Manager of the Weston, Clevedon & Portishead Railway offered to lend a petrol and a steam engine, both fully manned, to assist as required.

The station master at Llanvihangel, on strike since Tuesday, had had second thoughts and wished to return, but after some deliberation the superintendent was told not to re-engage him at present. At Hayes, striking staff threatened to refuse to feed the company's horses unless the signal box was closed, but the company decided to use volunteers to feed the horses, rather than be threatened.

A night inspector in the Exeter division appealed, with tears in his eyes, to be re-engaged 'having lost his nerve a bit on Tuesday, never having been on strike before'. He also was not allowed back for the present. Fresh instructions on the re-engagement of strikers were issued at 1 pm. Men could be re-engaged 'providing their services can be utilised in any capacity but no man who is known to have taken a leading part in organising or carrying out the strike, nor any supervisor, is to be allowed to resume duty without explicit instructions from this office' (i.e. HQ).

The driver 'arranged' for the 3.30 pm Paddington to Malvern told the London locomotive superintendent that the crossings at Ascott, Blockley and Campden were 'very uncertain' and that he understood one of the station masters had refused to open his crossing. The Worcester superintendent was asked to take the necessary action.

After some difficulties in providing the necessary engines, two banana specials left Avonmouth: one at 4.35 pm with 50 trucks for West Ealing (where it arrived at 10.38 pm - the consignment would be guarded overnight). The other special left at 5.30 pm for Reading with another 50 trucks, arriving there at 12.30 am (Sat).

Seventy-one volunteer signalmen were despatched to divisions needing them; this did not include Swansea as the latter said that he could manage 'in manning signal boxes by more or less qualified station masters and inspectors'.

Two United Dairies managers called personally at the Paddington offices in the afternoon to say that the GW was handling the milk traffic 'so satisfactorily' that various GW lorries, idle in Berkshire, Wiltshire and elsewhere could be withdrawn.

At 6 pm the Hotels Department rang to inform the SOL that the 10.15 am Cardiff to Paddington had run with a restaurant car, and requesting instructions for the return of the staff. They were advised to return with the 11.55 am ex-Paddington the next day, if possible.

The station masters at Little Mill and Usk had refused to signal a train over the Pontypool to Monmouth branch. The superintendent was instructed to ask the two men personally if they would deal with the train the next day; if they refused they were to be suspended.

In response to a direction to get the Torquay line open, the Exeter superintendent stated that he had only one signalman, and would need more before he could reopen the line. However he hoped to run an auto-train service of five return trips between Newton Abbot and Paignton starting on Monday, replacing the autos by normal trains when the service to Kingswear resumed, as soon as possible thereafter.

Saturday 8th May

The station master at Hereford, who only had one man to assist him, was having a particularly busy time - he was working *three* signal boxes involving a 2 mile walk for each train! A morning service from Worcester to Hereford was therefore declined (it may have run to Ledbury?).

The milk churn tally at Paddington was up on Wednesday's figure, some 2,580 churns being received between 6 pm, 7th May and 8 am, 8th May.

Since Friday efforts had been made to run a train of meat from Birkenhead to Paddington. The first problem was to get the vans in position for unloading; an engine was put out on Friday to do so, but was obstructed by strikers. The next problem was that the Shrewsbury superintendent wanted to close the line on Sunday to give the working men a rest. Finally the Birkenhead station master, supported by the Chester superintendent, felt that any attempt to move the meat by rail would lead to a riot. Both wanted the traffic to go by road. This was turning into another 'Milford fish' saga!

At 12 noon the General Manager (presumably) made his decision. All local opposition was brushed aside: the meat train must run. But this time it was not to be; the loading staff at Birkenhead Docks walked out and the train was cancelled.

Despite the Strike, Lord Glanely expected some trucks under load at Chippenham, and required for the Wiltshire Agricultural Show, to be dealt with. Bristol said this was not possible until a shunting engine could be found.

A remarkable combination of traincrew worked the 10.19 am special passenger from Cardiff to Paddington headed by locomotive 2925: Old Oak driver; Bullo Pill fireman; Carmarthen guard. The train left Cardiff with 114 passengers on board.

Mr Padmore at Exeter was still not off the hook so far as the Torquay line was concerned. Mr Nicholls did not accept the former's explanation that only one signalman was available 'as we are running trains in other divisions where the same position prevails'. Why weren't the station masters working the boxes? Mr Padmore replied that the level crossings were giving difficulty, but, two men having resumed, he was now able to run three trains from Newton Abbot

A busy suburban arrival unloads at Paddington platform 6 on 5th May, 1926 *Railway Gazette*

This crowd looks happy enough to have been photographed at a race course or other sports meeting. But it is actually part of a large crowd of strikers and their families being addressed by trade union leaders in the Park at Swindon, 8th May, 1926.

By permission of the National Museum of Labour History

A busy scene as volunteers deal with incoming milk traffic at Paddington. *GWR Magazine*

Platform 1 at Paddington is crowded with passengers and onlookers: one would hardly have imagined there was a strike on! *Courtesy GWR Musuem, Swindon*

The end of platforms 9/10 at Paddington on 11th May, 1926 with parcels lorries ready to leave with the day's deliveries. *Hulton Deutsch Collection Ltd*

to Kingswear and back, commencing Sunday.

On the staff front, an inspector at Old Oak Common, and two yard inspectors at Banbury and an inspector at Pengam ('an old Barry servant') would be allowed to return to work as shunters (at shunter's pay) if they were prepared to do so. (On Sunday the Banbury men accepted this offer, but not the Old Oak inspector; the Pengam man did not respond.) The station master at Severn Beach was supporting the strikers and was thus regarded as being on strike and required to give up the station keys.

Following much personal effort from (?HQ) inspector Partridge, who was down in Cornwall, a perishable special left Marazion at 9.47 am for Bristol and Paddington.

The only serious accident recorded in the pages of the SOL log happened this day. A morning auto-train from Oswestry to Gobowen had been worked by a 'driver' from the locomotive stores dept, piloted by the chief clerk to the divisional superintendent. On return to Oswestry, with driver and chief clerk in the leading carriage and fireman on the engine, it had been run into the bay platform, but had hit the stop blocks, run up the inclined rails forming the stop blocks and the leading carriage had demolished the end of the parcels office, finishing up inside it. None of the 40-50 passengers* in the vehicle had complained of injury, but the chief clerk was shaken and badly bruised. The cause was put down to a greasy rail (and presumably poor driving skills!). There were no company drivers or firemen working in the Oswestry division, all trains being worked by volunteers, more of whom were being sent down from London. The Ellesmere line reopened that morning.

In the evening an engine was derailed on catch points at Bristol West. Not far away at St Anne's Park a train had to be rescued after the engine failed, short of steam.

On orders received from the Ministry of Transport, the SS *St Helier* was required to proceed from Weymouth to Jersey and there embark one battalion of troops for England. The master would receive orders at Jersey as to whether further troops would be embarked at Guernsey (they were) and told his destination (Portsmouth).

Sunday 9th May

The 9.47 am (Sat) perishables from Marazion limped into Bristol Temple Meads at 12.10 am; it had had a bad run with the engine 'steaming badly'. It was to be recessed there until 8.30 am (it actually left at 9.49 am). Arrival time at Paddington is not recorded but a 9.25 am perishable from Marazion on Sunday fared rather better, arriving at Paddington at 11.19 pm the same day.

Plymouth reported that the Plymouth suburban service (Plympton-Saltash) had conveyed some 3,228 passengers on Saturday. They were attempting to clear the lines to Millbay Docks, at present congested with wagons, to enable boat trains to run (400 passengers were expected Wednesday off SS *Ranpura*).

Reading between the lines, it would appear that senior management had not

*A later memo reduced the number of passengers to 16, none of whom were in the front coach.

yet forgiven Mr Lea at Swansea for his telephone call last Thursday, following the 'Milford fish' incident. A telegram of rebuke was sent at midday Sunday asking why only one service was being worked in West Wales: why could not a service be instituted in the triangle Fishguard/Milford/Neyland/ Carmarthen? It ended, 'Swansea division worst on system'. Mr Lea responded with a list of trains run on the various branches (presumably on Sunday?) and the following passenger train agenda for Monday: Neyland-Carmarthen 4; Fishguard-Clarbeston Road 6; Tenby line 6; Cardigan 2; Newcastle Emlyn 4 (all chiefly with volunteers).

Soon afterwards Mr Lea fired off a telegram: 'Am pleased to say, commencing tomorrow, Block Telegraph working will be re-established on following sections: Fishguard & Goodwick-Clarbeston Rd; Neyland-Carmarthen Town: Swansea-Port Talbot; Whitland-Cardigan; Whitland-Pembroke Dock; Bronwydd Arms-Newcastle Emlyn'.

Advice was received after lunch that the St Ives branch would reopen on Monday, and so, it was hoped, would the Helston branch.

Weymouth was well provided with volunteers, and news came that some 23,000 packages of potatoes and tomatoes from the Channel Islands had been unloaded and despatched to various inland destinations on Saturday. Volunteers had worked the three steam and one electric cranes at the port, the latter being worked by an Admiral (presumably retired).

Reports came through this day of malicious acts carried out, firstly between Cradley and Old Hill 12 detonators had been placed on the down line and, after these were removed, 8 placed on the up line. It was decided to clip up and padlock the nearby catch point to prevent it being tampered with. A second incident occurred in the London area where the wire to the down main distant signal for Dawley, between Hayes and West Drayton, was cut.

The station master at Lydbrook Jn, on strike, advised of his wish to return to work but was not allowed to do so. A station inspector from Plymouth Millbay, and one from Slough, were not allowed to resume duty. Three yard foremen at Gloucester and a signalman at Kemble were allowed to return, but only on the understanding that they would work elsewhere, or do *any* work required of them.

Oswestry superintendent wired at 6 pm that he would be able to work all trains for which engines were available 'all over my district within limits of one shift'. All the relevant signal boxes were manned and sufficient guards were available. This, presumably, referred to preparations for Monday's train service.

Between 10.15 am, 8th May and 4 am, 9th May, no less than 7,613 churns of milk had been received at Paddington. Another 3,260 churns had arrived in Sunday daytime trains up to 7 pm.

The SS *St Helier*, conveying troops, left Jersey at 5.45 pm, Guernsey at 9 pm, and was expected at Portsmouth at 6 am Monday.

A circular (No. 3002) was received from the General Manager, and wired out to each superintendent, directing that because the injury to trading was expected to continue for some time, once 50 per cent of the normal complement of a station had resumed duty, any others taken on should only be re-engaged on the understanding that they 'are not relieved of the consequences of having broken your contract', and a record was to be kept of those employed on such terms (one assumes this would have allowed them to be sacked without notice if trade did not pick up).

Monday 10th May

The morning was occupied with advices of traffic to be moved currently, or anticipated. For example, on Wednesday the SS *Ranpura*, already expected, and the Blue Funnel SS *Sarpedon* would arrive at Plymouth at 6 am and there would be a total of 599 passengers to move to London. Later SS *Caika* was added to Wednesday's tally, with a further 165 passengers. Today, Monday, an Ocean Special left Plymouth at 12.30 pm carrying 350 passengers off SS *Ballarat*; this arrived at Paddington at 7.44 pm.

Talyllyn station master reported some minor vandalism at Llanvihangel Crossing between Trefeinon and Talyllyn. The 9 am passenger train from Brecon had run over six or seven stones placed on the line.

Swansea wired to express concern at the lack of engineering patrolling or police protection in certain parts of his division. Specifically, on the Burry Port & Gwendraeth Valley section, on which trains were not at present running, damage had been done at Trimsaran Road.

The GW had been trying to run trains to South Lambeth goods depot for several days, but the Southern Railway had been unable to man its signal boxes. The GW made another approach to the SR today, but the latter pointed out that even if the train ran it was unlikely that any deliveries by road could be effected. The SR was getting no deliveries out of Nine Elms depot because of 'mobs in adjoining streets'.

Presumably the movement of milk traffic was now considered routine because the log no longer mentions specific milk trains nor number of churns carried per 24 hours. But there is one entry this day: so much traffic was now passing that the SOL office rang the Chairman of United Dairies at 8.50 pm to say that Paddington milk platform was blocked with loaded cans, and a train with another 1,300 cans was waiting outside for space to be found to unload!

Lyons Cakes of Greenford enquired whether there was any prospect of a service for their staff and the London superintendent was asked to look into this.

Finally at 11.50 pm Mr Lea of Swansea telephoned to decline another offer from the SOL of 20 volunteer signalmen and the same number of guards. The area was in an inflammable state and he did not want to import men from London [who would have stood out like a sore thumb!]. The Civil Commissioner and the various Chief Constables agreed with him that it would be unwise 'to experiment in the way suggested' and he asked 'to be allowed to let things remain as they are' . . . he was manning signal boxes with his own men and doubtless others would return gradually. He was able to report that the Vale of Neath line would reopen as far as Glyn Neath tomorrow. There is no immediate response in the log to this request, but see Tuesday's extract for the eventual head office reaction.

A West of England 'express' loads up at Paddington's platform 2 on 11th May, 1926. *GWR Magazine*

A view down platform 1 at Paddington on 11th May, 1926. *GWR Magazine*

A poor picture but worth including because it indicates how busy Paddington remained during the Strike - platforms 1 and 2 are bustling in the afternoon of 10th May. *GWR Magazine*

The GWR's Kingswear-Dartmouth ferry *The Mew,* whose crews stopped work during the General Strike. This twin screw steamer had a long life, entering service in 1908 and continuing to maintain the short river crossing until 1954. *British Rail*

The GWR steamship *St Helier* which, as mentioned in Chapter Two, was kept so busy by the War Office that it was unable to carry out its normal duties of ferrying passengers and produce to and from the Channel Islands. This 1,885 ton vessel was introduced in 1925. She struck the pier at Jersey on 10th March, 1926 and was sent to her builders in Clydebank for repairs, only returning to service at the beginning of May. Built with two funnels, the second funnel, a dummy, was removed in 1928. This photograph was taken in August 1929, a year in which the *St Helier* worked the Channel Islands passenger service on her own for 29 weeks without a break. The vessel was withdrawn in 1960. *British Rail, courtesy Ian Coulson*

Tuesday 11th May

Worcester and Chester reported that the strike was still solid and, in fact, in the Chester division, no-one had reported for duty that morning. At a mass meeting in Liverpool on Monday, the city's MP had told the men to 'hold tight'.

There was a need to move food for the company's horses from Didcot Provender Stores to, variously, Paddington, Bristol, Newport, Cardiff and Hockley (Birmingham). The SOL office was able to quote goods services to the first four locations, but not for the moment to Hockley.

A call from Exeter division advised that the SS *Mew*, the company's Dartmouth ferry, had been withdrawn because the men were on strike. The River Dart Steamboat Company had offered to hire a vessel to the GWR, but as the independent ferry from Kingswear to Dartmouth, and the higher ferry from Britannia Crossing to Dartmouth were both running, and there were only four trains each way to/from Kingswear, the offer was declined.

The first train from Old Oak to South Lambeth left at noon. The yardmaster at Stewarts Lane covered the working of the boxes there and at Longhedge Jn. The trip returned at 5 pm and the log records that 'very useful work was performed'. The log remains silent as to whether road deliveries were possible.

At 1.25 pm came the reaction to Mr Lea's *cri-de-coeur* re volunteers: 4 shunters, 20 guards and 20 signalmen had been despatched to Swansea by the 8.55 and 11.55 am trains from Paddington 'with a request that Mr Lea make the best use of these men to improve the movement in the Swansea division'. As if to give the knife another turn, Swansea was also told that Mr Simpkins (the SOL's General Assistant) would be at Swansea tomorrow as 'Coordinating Officer'.*

Col Stephens (of light railway fame) telephoned at 2.30 pm to say that he had heard from Portmadoc (where he managed the Festiniog and the Welsh Highland Railway) that a good number of men were returning to work there and he thought the GW would like to know. On enquiry, Oswestry superintendent's office was unable to confirm this report.

A call from United Dairies requested that 500 churns of milk on hand at Paddington be moved to Aylesbury 'as the London supply appeared to be overdone'[!] The GWR was unable to co-operate as it had no service to Aylesbury, and the LNER was suffering a derailment at Neasden; it was suggested to UD that milk being loaded at Thame and Tiddington be diverted to Aylesbury.

The Road Transport department gave information of a GWR bus service between Gloucester and Cheltenham, to start tomorrow, Wednesday. At 5.20 pm the MP for Pembrokeshire wanted to know if it was intended to run another fish train from Milford to Paddington, and was told the matter was in hand. The Ministry of Transport suggested that the SS *St Helier*, which was oil burning, be used on the Channel Islands service rather than SS *Reindeer*, which was coal burning. However, as will be seen, the War Department hung on to it too long for the ship to be used as suggested.

In the evening the log gave details of staff reinstated to date:

*A team of HQ officers were appointed Coordinating Officers, one to each division, to assist local officers in the tricky business of reinstating strikers.

	Reinstated	*Not reinstated*
(prev. 24 hrs)		
7 am 10/5 - 7 am 11/5	208	56
Total since 3/5 - 7 am 11/5	406	132

indicating that 50 per cent of those re-employed had returned in the last 24 hrs.

Mr Lea at Swansea was in receipt of the following late evening personal telegram from Sir Felix Pole: 'Observe statement that 75 tons of fish conveyed by road from Milford yesterday. Surely you were not party to refusing this traffic?' (One feels sorry for Mr Lea, in the front line in a very volatile part of the system, but seemingly unable to do anything right as far as Paddington is concerned. Bearing in mind that he personally accompanied the Milford fish train last Wednesday, he obviously was not afraid to look trouble straight in the face.)

Wednesday 12th May

At 8.15 am, Sir William Price, on behalf of the Hyde Park Milk Pool ('Lake' would perhaps have been more appropriate) placed an embargo on milk from stations beyond a 100 mile radius of Paddington. He used the picturesque phrase that 'they had sufficient milk on hand to drown London'. However, when the GWR communicated with the Civil Commissioner on this matter, the latter asked that no action be taken for the present (outcome not recorded).

An enquiry of London division re the prospect of running to South Lambeth again, elicited the response that this would be impossible as Inspector Penny had been allotted to the LMS company today. It transpired that Inspector Penny was the only person able to work the GWR signal boxes and was, in effect, the human train staff. However, it was hoped to run to Stewarts Lane and Shepherds Bush tomorrow.

Further to the last telegram to Mr Lea, it is possible that the latter in his reply referred to the lack of police protection in the area because the log records an 11.35 am conversation with the GW Supt of Police, the latter confirming having spoken personally with the Chief Constable of Carmarthenshire who had assured him that 'the company was free to run trains between Swansea and Carmarthen and that adequate protection would be afforded'.

This entry was followed by a conversation with Mr Lea at 12.30 pm. The previous assurance was conveyed to him; Mr Lea said that he was running a goods train conveying foodstuffs from Swansea to Llanelly today (*which he would accompany personally*). He had endeavoured to arrange a fish train from Milford today, but without success (perhaps there was no traffic). However, one would run tomorrow, and daily thereafter.

A 'DIY' branchline operation is recorded at 12.53 pm, shown here verbatim:

> Wire from Hungerford - Sir Francis Burdett asked for leave to open the line from Marlborough High Level to Savernake Low Level. Has obtained volunteer engine driver and fireman. Engine driver would like trial trip or instruction first. He left Royal Engineers at end of war.
> (outcome not recorded)

At about 1.15 pm the radio broadcast the news that, at a meeting at 10, Downing Street, Mr Pugh, on behalf of the TUC, announced that the General Strike would be terminated today. All superintendents were asked to apply circular 3002 conditions (see Sunday) to *all* men resuming from now on.

It was, at first, anticipated that a maximum of 50 per cent of passenger trains would run on Thursday, and goods trains as necessary, priority being given to foodstuffs and perishables already on hand.

There was an early response from the public to the broadcast, despite the Strike not ending until midnight. By 5.15 pm some 260 tons of foodstuffs had been brought into Paddington Goods by private vehicles, and it was still arriving. However, the chief goods manager was informed, it would be impossible to move any of this before 6 am tomorrow, at the earliest.

A precautionary wire was sent out at 7.30 pm to all superintendents suggesting that all signalmen should be reinstated, but volunteers should not be released until replaced by regular men. Volunteers in other grades should similarly not be released if still required.

The terms under which the men should be reinstated was causing trouble and from 7.30 pm onwards there was a stream of messages reflecting this. Acton Yard inspectors and shunters refused to accept the form intimating that they had broken their contract; so in quick succession did staff at Reading, Maidenhead and, later, Old Oak. Staff at Didcot, Taunton, Minehead, Exeter, Torre, Churston, Kingswear, St Blazey, Millbay, Croes Newydd and Swansea would only return if *all* their number were taken back on.

The early optimism of a 50 per cent passenger service had now evaporated, and, at 9.55 pm, superintendents were told to repeat today's programme 'with such additions as circumstances permit'.

At Oswestry, where enginemen had been out to a man, those men, and traffic department staff, were prepared to report for duty as required (i.e. when the company called for them). At Cardiff, however, where the Asst SOL, Mr Wilkinson, met a deputation from all the Trade Unions, the men refused the conditions and would not return to work.

Thursday 13th May

Matters continued in a similar vein into the early hours. In Birmingham division, the response was rather mixed. Signalmen would not accept the conditions of circular 3002, while enginemen at Stafford Road (and Chester) were returning to work. Henley in Arden NUR branch had been told by Unity House not to sign any document (it was necessary to sign for receipt of 3002). Banbury staff passed a resolution claiming victimisation of staff returning to work.

As it became apparent that staff would not sign for circular 3002, it became necessary to ring the General Manager (at 1.30 am); the latter stated that the main thing was to get the men back to work. Thereafter the superintendents were told to emphasise to the men that the strike had been called off unconditionally, 'and it is up to them to return to work'. The conditions of

GREAT WESTERN RAILWAY

NOTICE

The Railway Companies announce that arrangements are being made to increase their train services at the earliest practicable moment, but the injury to trade is believed to be so serious that for some time full pre-strike services will not be required. All men who can be employed immediately are being accepted for duty and others will be accepted as soon as possible, subject to two conditions:—

(1) Every man who left his work without notice has broken his contract of service and the Companies feel they must reserve any rights they possess in this matter.

(2) A number of men in positions of trust have gone on strike, and others have been guilty of acts of violence and intimidation.

The Companies propose to examine these cases individually and meanwhile they reserve their decision in regard to them.

The Companies feel compelled to make these reservations in regard to the re-instatement of staff in the interests of the public and to safeguard future peace and discipline on the Railways.

The Companies take the opportunity to state that rumours that have been circulated to the effect that they are refusing to take men back except at wage reductions are absolutely incorrect.

FELIX J. C. POLE
General Manager.

Paddington Station,
May 13th, 1926.

The company's reservations about reinstatement of strikers.

circular 3002 still applied, and the men must understand these terms, even if they would not sign for them.

A round-up at 6 am of freight trains proposed in each division revealed the general statement that locomen were not returning to work, even at Oswestry. In the Worcester and Chester divisions the number of pickets had been increased. At Oxley Sidings 23 staff had reported, at Birmingham Snow Hill, 15 and at Hatton, 3, but only 2 at Snow Hill would accept the circular and had been allowed to restart.

A summary of staff resuming in the 24 hours up to 9 am showed a very small improvement:

Clerical	12
Supervisory	4
Guards	30
Signalmen	52
Shunters	11
Others	79
Total	188

The signalmen on the West London line would not resume duty until one of their number at Kensington was reinstated.

At 12.15 pm the GPO advised that they would resume forwarding parcels post but would need longer to resume the overnight TPO services.

A message came from Gloucester at lunchtime that no staff had presented themselves for duty today, and a resolution had been passed last night that staff would only resume *en bloc*. It was suggested that the overnight services between South Wales-Paddington and vice versa (via Gloucester) should not run, as the LMS could not man Standish Jn, Haresfield, Naas Crossing or Tramway Crossing signal boxes (one assumes these trains had been reinstated under the earlier, optimistic 50 per cent train service plan).

After lunch a notice setting out the company's terms for reinstatement (*illustrated*) was telephoned, and afterwards distributed, to all superintendents, and the press. It had become apparent that the Unions had interpreted the word 'unconditional' in the company's announcement of the end of the Strike as being unconditional on *both* sides. A message had gone out from Unity House that morning along the lines of 'one back, all back'. (Following receipt of these terms (the terms expressed in the GWR poster, *illustrated*, were used by all the companies), all three Trade Unions notified, that afternoon, their intention of continuing the Railwaymen's Strike.)

Two yard inspectors at Hackney, Newton Abbot were allowed back as shunters, but retained their inspector's rate of pay.

Just before 10 pm came information of a pannier tank derailed at Old Oak Common East. It had been proceeding from the yard to shed, but passed a signal at danger and became derailed on a catch point leading off the down engine line. The breakdown gang from Southall had been sent for.

The last two return journeys between Pontypool Road and Nelson had had to be withdrawn because of stone throwing incidents at Pontllanfraith, Treowen and Hafodyrynys.

Friday 14th May

The marine superintendent at Weymouth rang soon after midnight to say that the SS *St Helier*, which had been at Portsmouth since Monday morning, had still not been released by the War Office. Capt. Langdon, the master, had been reporting three times a day to the Admiral Superintendent since arrival, but the latter had received no instructions to dispense with his services. The GWR wanted the ship to return to Weymouth and a call was made to the Ministry of Transport to ask for that to be arranged. (It was released at 9.30 am and ETA Weymouth was 3.30 pm.)

Milk received at Paddington the previous day had totalled 7,013 churns, plus 120 tons of fish and 200 boxes asparagus (from Worcester).

The 7 am staff position showed that matters were worse than yesterday. In the London division, at Didcot and Oxford, for example, less staff reported than on the previous day. In Bristol, Exeter and Swansea divisions staff would only return *en bloc*. An update from Birmingham stated that 55 men had applied for reinstatement yesterday, but only four signalmen accepted the form. Oxley Sidings and Stourbridge Jn men had decided to stay out.

In Chester division no men had reported today. He also advised that the Mersey Railway (not GWR) had commenced a full service yesterday, but all the men had now gone back on strike. Birmingham, however, could report an improvement later that morning; men were subscribing to the conditions and he had 30 sets of trainmen available.

At about 10.15 am a train ran over a piece of metal placed on the down main line at Hanwell.

Mr Simpkins phoned in from Swansea at 11.05 am to report that the 10 am from Swansea to West Wales had run this morning. It had stopped at Llanelly to unload parcels for 10 minutes and no trouble had occurred. The booking office there was being manned by a relief clerk and things 'appear to be going all right'. There would be another five trains through Llanelly today, including the Milford fish train this afternoon (it left Milford at 1 pm).

The SOL log recorded that London Underground had reached agreement at 2.30 am and men would be returning to duty the next day, Saturday. All the station staff would be taken back and 75 per cent of the train staff, the remainder as traffic developed.

At 4.15 pm the office of the Civil Commissioner telephoned that a settlement had been reached with the railway unions, and duly signed and sealed. The terms (*see Chapter Eight*) were notified to all superintendents, and that circular 3002 was now cancelled.

Following a personal telegram of congratulations to each superintendent from Mr Nicholls, they were then exhorted to run a special passenger service over the weekend, not exceeding 50 per cent of the normal service, and a 50 per cent service from Monday onwards. On the freight side, they were to spend the weekend 'squaring up' the yards and forming trains, running booked trains if traffic was available.

The message that *all* staff would not be taken back straightaway had still not got through. London division advised that the NUR had wired their branches,

'Complete reinstatement secured without penalties. All members should report for duty immediately.' As a result, staff at Kensington and Southall, who had assumed that they would all be taken back, had to have the terms explained to them by their respective station masters.

Saturday 15th May-Monday 17th May

A 2.30 am (Sat) round-up of the staff position revealed little difficulty arising, but at Swindon and Yeovil men would not accept the conditions laid down. At Newton Abbot the men proposed 'to march to work in a body today'. At Swansea Docks (am Sunday) the men said they would not return unless all the men were reinstated.

At 3 pm Sunday, Exeter rang to say that the SS *Mew* would be unavailable until Thursday for boiler cleaning and wished to hire from the River Dart Steamboat Co. However, Exeter was told to carry on as before (i.e. no service).

The 'news' recorded over this final weekend was very thin, and Monday morning's entries mainly relate to traffic to/from the LNER. The last entry in this very interesting account of the General Strike's effect on the GWR is timed at 9.30 am, Monday 17th May.

A train leaving Paddington station platform 2 during the Strike.

Hulton Deutsch Collection Ltd

Statistics

Number of Passenger, Milk and Perishable Trains and Mileage Run on the GWR

24 hrs ended 9 pm	*No. of Trains*	*Total Mileage*	*Normal Mileage*	*% of Normal Mileage*
4th May*	392	11,357	103,444	11.00
5th May	194	7,294	103,444	7.05
6th May	353	9,731	103,444	9.41
7th May	479	12,537	103,444	12.12
8th May	612	14,956	103,444	14.46
9th May (Sun)	492	12,853	28,449	45.18
10th May	908	19,568	92,729	21.10
11th May	1,022	22,161	103,444	21.42
12th May	1,170	25,294	103,444	24.45
13th May	1,213	26,520	103,444	25.64
14th May	1,245	28,161	103,444	27.24

Number of Freight Trains and Mileage Run

24 hrs ended 9 pm	*No. of Trains*	*Total Mileage*	*Normal Mileage*	*% of Normal Mileage*
4th May*	101	4,035	73,000	5.52
5th May	8	275	73,000	0.38
6th May	17	573	73,000	0.79
7th May	30	1,216	73,000	1.67
8th May	47	2,099	73,000	2.88
9th May (Sun)	53	1,569	10,950	14.33
10th May	93	3,321	62,050	5.35
11th May	134	4,677	73,000	6.41
12th May	128	4,226	73,000	5.79
13th May	138	4,385	73,000	6.01
14th May	147	5,652	73,000	7.74

* - including three hours pre-Strike period

A view taken in 1926, after the General Strike ended, but before the miners returned to work. The *Jevington Court*, owned by the Court Line of London discharges imported coal into a line of GWR locomotive coal wagons in Newport's North Dock. *Welsh Industrial & Maritime Museum*

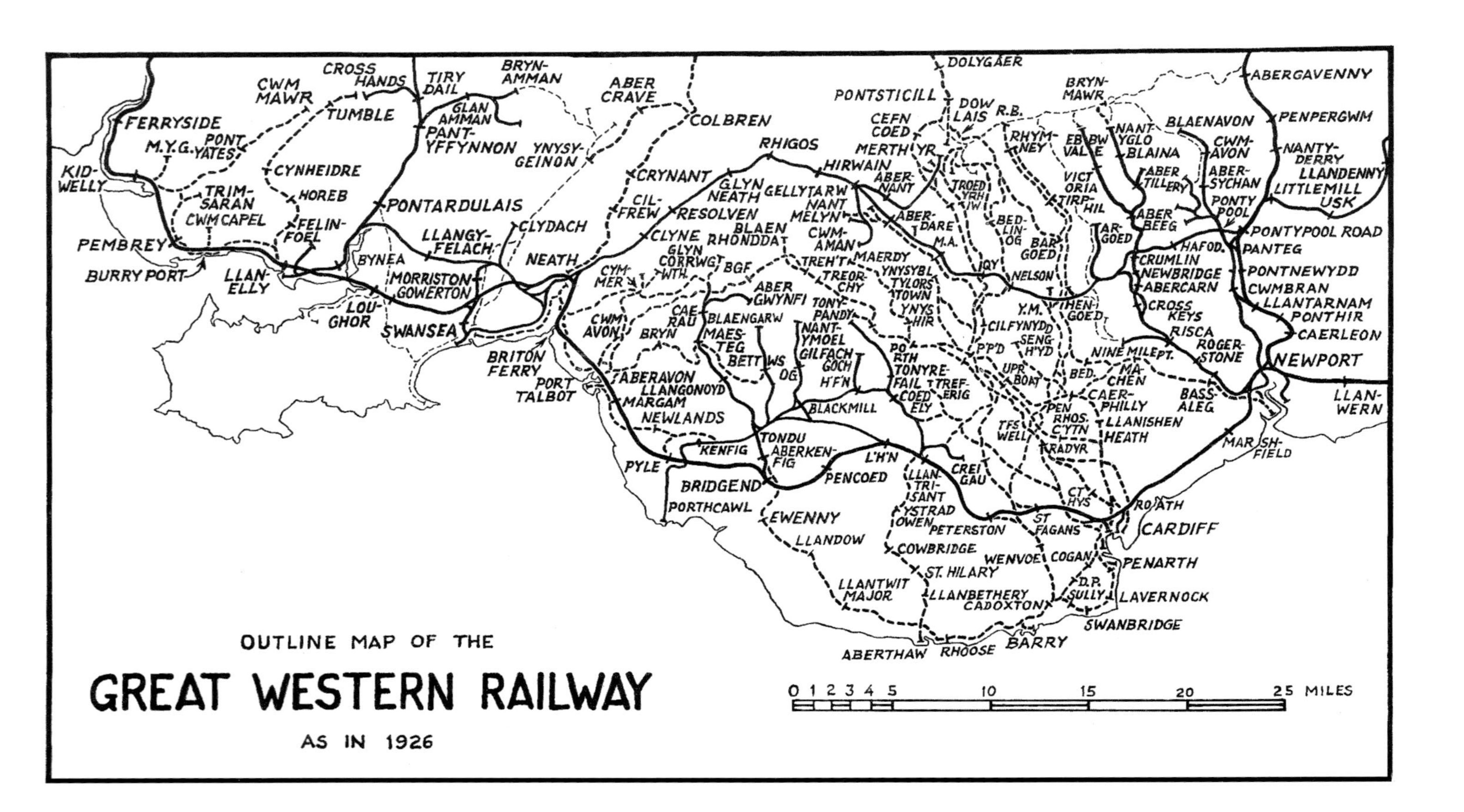
OUTLINE MAP OF THE
GREAT WESTERN RAILWAY
AS IN 1926
0 1 2 3 4 5 10 15 20 25 MILES
KIDWELLY
FERRYSIDE
M.Y.G.
PONT YATES
CWM MAWR
CROSS HANDS
TUMBLE
TIRY DAIL
BRYNAMMAN
GLAN AMMAN
PANTYFFYNNON
YNYSYGEINON
ABER CRAVE
COLBREN
CYNHEIDRE
HOREB
TRIMSARAN
CWMCAPEL
FELINFOEL
PEMBREY
BURRY PORT
LLANELLY
PONTARDULAIS
LLANGYFELACH
BYNEA
MORRISTON
GOWERTON
LOUGHOR
SWANSEA
CLYDACH
NEATH
BRITON FERRY
PORT TALBOT
CRYNANT
CILFREW
RESOLVEN
CLYNE
GLYN NEATH
RHIGOS
HIRWAIN
GELLYTARW
NANT MELYN
CWMAMAN
BLAEN RHONDDA
GLYN CORRWG
BGF
CYMMER
WTH.
CWM AVON
CAE RAU
BRYN
ABERAVON
LLANGONOYD
MARGAM
NEWLANDS
PYLE
KENFIG
PORTHCAWL
BRIDGEND
ABERGWYNFI
BLAENGARW
MAESTEG
BETTWS
OG
TONDU
ABERKENFIG
BLACKMILL
NANTYMOEL
GILFACH GOCH
H'F'N
TONYPANDY
TREH'T
MAERDY
TREORCHY
YNYSYBL
TYLORS TOWN
YNYSHIR
PORTH
TONYREFAIL
TREFERIG
COED ELY
L'H'N
PENCOED
LLANTRISANT
CREIGAU
EWENNY
LLANDOW
YSTRAD OWEN
PETERSTON
COWBRIDGE
ST. HILARY
LLANTWIT MAJOR
LLANBETHERY
CADOXTON
ABERTHAW
RHOOSE
BARRY
SWANBRIDGE
LAVERNOCK
SULLY
D.P.
COGAN
WENVOE
PENARTH
CARDIFF
ROATH
ST FAGANS
CT HYS
RADYR
TFS WELL
PEN RHOS. C'YTN
HEATH
LLANISHEN
CAERPHILLY
BED.
MACHEN
UPR BOAT
P'P'D
SENG H'YD
CILFYNYDD
Y.M.
YHENGOED
NINE MILE PT.
RISCA
ROGERSTONE
CROSS KEYS
BASSALEG
MARSHFIELD
NEWPORT
LLANWERN
CAERLEON
PONTHIR
LLANTARNAM
CWMBRAN
PONTNEWYDD
PANTEG
PONTYPOOL ROAD
PONTY POOL
ABERSYCHAN
CWMAVON
BLAENAVON
PENPERGWM
ABERGAVENNY
NANTYDERRY
LLANDENNY
LITTLEMILL
USK
HAFOD.
CRUMLIN
NEWBRIDGE
ABERCARN
ABER BEEG
ABER TILLERY
NANTYGLO
BLAINA
BRYNMAWR
EBBW VALE
ARGOED
VICTORIA
TIRPHIL
RHYMNEY
BED LINOG
BARGOED
NELSON
QY
M.A.
ABERDARE
ABERNANT
TROED YRHIW
MERTHYR
CEFN COED
DOWLAIS
R.B.
PONTSTICILL
DOLYGAER

Chapter Three

Strike Strongly Supported: Cardiff Close Down

The Cardiff division made a comprehensive record of divisional happenings during the General Strike. This is filed at the Public Record Office (RAIL250/777) and forms the basis of this chapter.

The Strike was very strongly supported in this division and no less than 86 per cent of the traffic staff (these excluded drivers and firemen etc.) struck from the outset, a percentage which only moved up or down by no more than one percentage point for the duration of the Strike. This compared with a GWR average for traffic staff on strike of between 72-77 per cent. In some grades staff *working* barely reached double figures; e.g. on 4th May 7 guards out of 895, 11 signalmen out of 809 and 4 shunters out of 355 were at work, and whilst these particular grades mirrored GWR trends, in the case of the clerical staff feelings ran much higher here than elsewhere. GWR-wide about 25 per cent of the clerical staff struck*, but in the Cardiff division over 47 per cent of the clerks were on strike on 4th May. Although this worsened somewhat to 53 per cent on strike on 8th May, it had moved back to just over 50 per cent not at work when the Strike ended on 14th May. A table showing the number of staff *on duty* throughout the Strike is printed later in this Chapter. Four station masters struck, those at Caerphilly, Pengam, Blackmill and Southerndown Road; the latter resumed duty almost immediately but the others were absent throughout, although the Blackmill man did ask to resume on 10th May but his request was declined. There is no evidence (from the staff changes columns of the *GWR Magazine* that any of these men afterwards were demoted but SM Caerphilly was certainly 'on the list' (*see Chapter Eight*).

Use of volunteers was quite light in this division, initially only 13 retired employees and 31 other volunteers being employed. These were aided by redeployment of GWR staff remaining on duty who 'readily offered to perform any duties required' and acted as signalmen, guards or porters etc. as requested. On the evening of 7th May, ten volunteer signalmen, who had been trained at Royal Oak, arrived from London. After a couple of days getting acclimatised five were placed in 'light duty' boxes, viz Penarth Station, East Branch Jn, Radyr Jn and Ely Paper Mills. Two others were sent to Cogan Station box and Cadoxton South and the remaining three were sent to assist in Newtown West, Long Dyke and Rumney River Bridge boxes. Later four trained volunteer guards and a shunter from London were usefully employed. Volunteers and employees who could not get home were accommodated at Cardiff General, Queen Street and Llantrisant, and the refreshment rooms at Cardiff General were kept open continuously for the use of the staff during the Strike.

On the morning of 4th May, there were no less than 3,345 wagons on hand in the various Cardiff yards, many of which were for Swansea, West Wales and the Valley towns. As shunting power became available over the next few days,

*It should be noted that the percentage of clerks and supervisors on strike in the other three big companies was much closer to 45% than the GWR's 25%.

wagons containing perishables were segregated and placed in position for unloading, a total of 640 wagons being so dealt with. Consignees at towns and villages outside Cardiff were advised and, where possible, came and collected their goods from Cardiff. A limited number of goods trains were run to Swansea, Gloucester, Pontypool Road etc., even one cattle train to London, but the total number of goods trains organised by the Cardiff Division only came to 71.

The handling of passenger traffic was more successful: on the first day it was only possible to run two trains but this figure improved day by day until on the last day of the emergency 111 trains were run. From 6th May onwards quite reasonable local services were run between Radyr (later Taff's Well) and Penarth via Cardiff, Cardiff and Llanishen and (from 7th May) Cardiff and Whitchurch. From 10th May Barry and Porthcawl were added to the list of destinations served. The summarised position is as follows:

	'Through Trains'	*Local Trains*	*Total*
4th May	2		2
5th May	4		4
6th May	12	11	23
7th May	14	29	43
8th May	18	35	53
9th May (Sun)	17	29	46
10th May	16	39	55
11th May	18	54	72
12th May	17	64	81
13th May	18	64	82
14th May	23	64	87
15th May	23	88	111

On Monday 17th May practically a normal passenger service was run between 6 am and 10 pm, but as the miners' strike was continuing services were reduced to 50 per cent of normal from 21st May, so as to conserve coal. The service between Cowbridge and Aberthaw (Low Level) was entirely suspended. The full *winter* train service was introduced on 12th July, except that the Cowbridge-Aberthaw service remained suspended.

Block signalling was maintained between Newtown West and Penarth Jn (Cardiff) during the whole period when trains were running, and from 10th May block working was extended to the whole of the main line, and from 11th May to all sections where trains were running. Temporary block switches were installed in Maindy Bridge and Queen Street Station signal boxes on 10th May, enabling these boxes to switch out if necessary.

The gates of the level crossings situated on the main line (i.e. Llantrisant West, Miskin, Pontsarn and Canton) were secured across the road at the beginning of the Strike, and remained in that position until it was possible to man the adjacent signal box.

There were five cases of 'intimidation' of non-striking staff during the stoppage, one of which (a signalman at Bridgend) led to the ultimate dismissal of the two perpetrators (although they were reinstated on appeal). The other four cases (at Rhymney (RR), Pontlottyn, Tirphil and Dowlais) all concerned public demonstrations or deputations seeking to persuade station masters to leave their posts. All except Rhymney remained at their stations.

Some minor damage was done to property: on 5th May 50 keys were removed from a 100 yds-long section south of Pontypridd tunnel (Barry section); on 7th May the wire to Penarth Curve South down inner home signal was cut, and the next day at the same location a point detection box was damaged. The report notes that while special constables did their best to patrol the lines of the division, 'practically the whole of the Engineering Department were strikers'.

After the Strike ended, the division found itself, for the first time, as a large scale *importer* of coal for locomotive purposes. The first shipload arrived on 14th June and from then until the end of the year 101 cargoes varying between 2,000-11,000 tons, chiefly from America, were discharged at Cardiff, Penarth or Barry. In total, no less than 614,297 tons of GW locomotive coal were received. To move this, locomotive coal wagons, common user and even hired colliery wagons had to be pressed into service; it is recorded that as many as 25 special trains were run in one day.

As well as the Great Western coal, 28 steamers discharged locomotive coal for the LMSR, totalling 185,200 tons in the same period.

On Monday 17th May when striking staff resumed duty and 'normal' services restarted, it was not possible to reinstate all former staff, because of the loss of traffic and the continuing miners' strike.

	Permanent Staff At Work During Strike	*Men Reinstated on 17th May*	*Men For Whom no Employment found on 17th May*
Clerical	271	189	67
Supervisory	166	37	13
Guards	11	312	572
Signalmen	28	506	275
Shunters	6	175	174
Other Grades (excl. drivers/firemen)	115	693	455
	597	1912	1556 (31%)

This position continued practically unchanged until 1st June when the Guaranteed Week was suspended and a system of job sharing introduced for as many men as possible, so as to equalise weekly earnings at approximately three days pay.

With the suspension of the Guaranteed Week and by booking as many of those staff entitled to holidays with pay as possible on annual leave during the period of suspension, significant financial savings in wages were made for the remainder of the year, as the following table shows.

Suspension of Guaranteed Week - Particulars of Staff Savings - Cardiff Division (Traffic Dept)

Week Ended	*No. of Staff actually employed full time*	*No. on Annual Leave*	*No. of Staff employed part time*	*Average week-days worked*	*No. Not employed*	*No. absent through Sickness*	*TOTAL*	*No of full time staff to which No. employed is equivalent Excl. staff on Ann. Leave*	*Percentage of normal staff employed*	*Authorised Staff Establishment*	*Savings*		
											£	*s.*	*d.*
June 12th	1836	773	1126	3.41	394		4129	2477	59	4129	2517	11	8
June 19th	1715	723	1329	3.40	362		4129	2470	59	4129	2672	16	1
June 26th	1492	469	1837	3.33	468	63	4129	2399	58	4129	3653	18	1
July 3rd	1425	284	1815	3.33	539	65	4129	2431	59	4129	4067	4	11
July 10th	1389	228	1908	3.33	568	66	4129	2424	59	4129	4287	9	5
July 17th	1404	165	1973	3.36	529	58	4129	2508	60	4129	4245	8	5
July 24th	1440	134	1992	3.37	513	50	4129	2558	61	4129	4197	0	6
July 31st	1435	102	2012	3.35	525	55	4129	2560	62	4129	4284	5	11
Aug. 8th	1439	83	2096	3.35	450	61	4129	2608	63	4129	4178	14	4
Aug. 15th	1381	94	2060	3.35	531	63	4129	2534	61	4129	4327	16	5
Aug. 22nd	1400	93	2049	3.37	522	65	4129	2553	61	4129	4287	11	0
Aug. 29th	1429	76	2044	3.38	518	68	4129	2582	62	4129	4205	16	4
Sep. 5th	1365	58	2090	3.46	557	59	4129	2571	62	4129	4338	0	2
Sep. 12th	1359	64	2087	3.50	555	64	4129	2576	62	4129	4344	1	3
Sep. 19th	1330	50	2137	3.46	551	61	4129	2567	62	4129	4389	19	0
Sep. 26th	1305	44	2166	3.47	559	55	4129	2558	62	4129	4407	1	5
Oct. 3rd	1251	31	2230	3.53	557	60	4129	2562	62	4129	4435	3	5
Oct. 10th	1262	26	2211	3.40	564	66	4129	2562	62	4129	4422	17	8
Oct. 17th	1217	22	2265	3.50	551	74	4129	2561	62	4129	4467	13	7
Oct. 24th	1232	18	2250	3.56	554	75	4129	2568	62	4129	4451	18	6
Oct. 31st	1253	9	2251	3.54	541	75	4129	2582	62	4129	4445	4	5
Nov. 6th	1222	4	2296	3.54	520	87	4129	2580	62	4129	4424	4	9
Nov. 13th	1303	11	2219	3.50	504	92	4129	2605	63	4129	4565	6	8
Nov. 20th	1324	9	2217	3.55	486	93	4129	2636	63	4129	4235	2	5
Nov. 27th	1353	10	2207	3.57	476	83	4129	2667	64	4129	4197	7	7
Dec. 5th	1390	4	2231	3.57	418	86	4129	2720	66	4129	4059	10	5
Dec. 12th	1920	17	1940	3.91	171	81	4129	3186	77	4129	2590	18	6
Dec. 19th	2323	18	1584	4.22	126	78	4129	3439	83	4129	1872	19	9
Dec, 25th	3004	18	930	4.12	103	74	4129	3644	89	4129	1268	4	8
								TOTAL SAVINGS			113640	6	10

Blackmill station, in South Wales, one of those whose station master decided to go on strike. The station master was in class 4 and he had a staff of 10 signalmen, porters and gatemen, but no clerical staff. In 1926 staff costs were £1,024 and traffic receipts only £1,436. *Lens of Sutton*

Bristol West signal box, worked during the Strike first by a divisional inspector and later a retired chief inspector. The box was swept away in 1935 when the GWR introduced power signalling to Bristol. The engine is 'Saint' class 4-6-0 No. 2986 *Robin Hood* built in 1905 and withdrawn in 1932. *HMRS*

Chapter Four

Struggling to Keep Going: Bristol Division Strike Diary

The Bristol superintendent, Mr H.R. Griffiths, sent a daily report of Strike happenings contemporaneously to the superintendent of the line. This is filed at PRO Kew under reference RAIL253/546. It may well be that some of the other superintendents also did so, but, apart from the Cardiff Division report written after the Strike (*see Chapter Three*), they appear no longer to be available. Much archive material was, of course, lost during World War II, either as a result of wartime bombing or because paper was sent for salvage.

Much of the information concerned trains planned and run and, as these feature in other chapters, they will not be referred to again here.

Tuesday 4th/Early Wednesday 5th May

Many signalmen who had commenced their night turn of duty on 3rd May remained at work until the end of their shift, but some of the 'principal boxes' were deserted. At Bristol East the signalmen 'put the gas out and left the box at midnight.' However, the chief divisional signalling inspector took duty in the box soon afterwards, relit the gas and remained there for the rest of the night and *all the next day*. Other important boxes were staffed by district inspectors and 'a fair number of trains were dealt with during the night.'

On 5th May the historian E.T. MacDermot of Minehead, who was then engaged in writing the history of the GWR (published in 1927), was taken on as a signalman at Bristol South Wales Jn box, 'as he did on the occasion of a former strike' [probably 1919]. A retired chief signalling inspector worked Bristol West box, assisted by Mr Griffiths' personal clerk. A retired signalman was placed in North Somerset Jn box. At Weston-super-Mare the station master was working both boxes, as mentioned in Chapter Two.

Some station masters had walked out. A booking office clerk from Bristol was sent to take charge of Corsham; in an ironic twist the former station master was reduced to booking clerk at Bristol after the Strike. The goods clerk at Wantage Road was sent to replace the station master at Steventon; the Wantage Road station master made arrangements for the two level crossings at Steventon to be covered.

This record reveals where Mr C.R. Clinker was first sent as a staff volunteer (*see Chapter Five*): 'The station master at Codford is reported being in a nervous condition and Mr Clinker, a clerk in this office, has been sent out by motor car to prop him up.'

Milk traffic offered had been disposed of by the very limited train service except for 'a few churns from Highbridge which had to be disposed of at Bristol for want of a service forward.'

On 4th May, out of a total divisional traffic staff (i.e. excluding footplate staff etc.) of 3,326, 2,241 were on strike 'as far as could be ascertained.'

On the morning of 5th May the only staff footplate crews available were five sets at Westbury, plus two volunteers and four sets at Swindon. In the case of the Swindon sets, the firemen were 'pupils' [i.e. apprentices at Swindon Works].

Also on 5th May the guard of the 8.25 am Wells-Bristol reported that he had had to set the points at Axbridge for his train, the station master having declined to do so. The guard was told that he could pass over the 'wrong' line on his return journey, if necessary, as his was the only train on the branch.

Wednesday 5th/Early Thursday 6th May

Six hours shunting was performed at Kingsland Road and Temple Meads Goods, placing wagons for unloading. An HQ travelling goods train inspector and a divisional goods inspector had refused to assist in this work on the grounds that there were resident inspectors on duty in these yards who had refused to carry out the work. In the event 'Mr Lampitt [goods agent] and his assistant Mr Humphrey' performed the shunting. A goods train from Acton at 3 pm had detached traffic at Swindon and Temple Meads Goods.

The number of staff on strike was 2,409 out of 3,326. Additional volunteers had been taken on to man Pilning Jn signal box: the retired station master from Pilning and a retired Severn Tunnel inspector. Also, a Mr Gordon Roe of Pill had offered his services and had been sent to Portishead to learn the signal box there, despite the branch being at present closed. The division was, in fact, making strenuous efforts to open the branch as petrol was shipped in to Portishead for forwarding in tank cars.

Mr Griffiths concluded his report by saying that it was not sensible to take on more 'traffic' (rather than 'locomotive') volunteers until more engines could be made available for use and that this was the key issue.

Thursday 6th/Early Friday 7th May

Despite the working of a special from Portishead with 17 petrol tanks for Birmingham, the volunteer there had asked to be released to join the Police Auxiliary and this had been agreed. A special goods train had run from Bruton to Bristol Lawrence Hill; this had been formed of the 11.35 pm Paddington-Newton Abbot freight of 3rd May which had terminated at Bruton.

The superintendent said that he was investigating the actions of the Wells station master, who, on 4th May, should have done more to release a GWR engine trapped at Wells behind the level crossing gates of the Somerset & Dorset signal box which was not being worked. Presumably it was considered that he should have opened the box to enable the engine to be recovered.

Several cases of intimidation were listed, including that of the signalman at Pylle Hill Junction who said that his wife had been molested.

Additional volunteers taken on included (retired) inspector Treasure, employed in Bath signal box, and a station master retired from Clifton Down. The two volunteers for Pilning Jn box were now less willing, as the staff on duty there, including the station master, had threatened to walk out if they took duty. At Ludgershall seven men on strike desired to return, but as no trains were running between Swindon and Andover Jn, they had been asked if they were prepared to work elsewhere.

At 7 am on 7th May the number of staff on strike was 2,448.

Friday 7th May

Shunting engines had been employed at Temple Meads, East Depot and Swindon and 'a considerable number' of wagons positioned for unloading. A simple statement, but it should not be assumed that this had been easy to arrange; one can only guess at the effort put into raising steam in these engines, finding crews for them, and, finally, shunters sufficiently competent to work with them in the yards.

Twenty men had returned to duty, mostly on the M&SWJ section. To date, of 189 volunteers registered only 29 had been taken on. The employment of volunteers was regulated by the limited number of engines (and men) available for use.

There had been two cases of inexperienced enginemen getting into difficulties. Both cases had occurred in Clifton Down tunnel, a banana special and a passenger train stalling, causing considerable delay. 'These cases indicate the care which has to be taken in putting inexperienced men to work over lines with steep gradients and other conditions about which the men have practically no knowledge.'

The retired guard working the 5.15 pm Bristol to Avonmouth had reported stones thrown at the train at Shirehampton and some of the Bristol Yard signalmen had to be escorted home after duty.

Saturday 8th May

The goods clerk from Wantage Road, who had been in charge at Steventon, today went on strike, probably 'blowing' any future chance of being promoted. The station master at Severn Beach, which was at present closed, had refused to take duty in Bristol and was therefore regarded as on strike. (This man was not allowed to resume duty until 19th June, after being interviewed by the General Manager and having given an undertaking that he would comply with such an instruction in future.) However, five men had returned to duty.

A driver shunting at Bristol, West Sidings had misread a signal and become derailed. A Bath to Bristol train had stalled in St Anne's Park tunnel and had to be pushed by another train. A Portishead train had been stoned near Bedminster, and the windows of Ashton Swing Bridge signal box had been broken.

Mr Griffiths concluded with his familiar lament re shortage of enginemen. To work the usual traffic of the division 370 sets of enginemen were required:*

*If 'set' here means driver & fireman (the usual meaning of the term), then why under Monday 10th May does the diary declare 370 engines as the daily requirement also? One of these figures must be wrong; in fact a staff census for March 1925 indicates that there were 754 sets in the division then.

today they had just 35 sets, consisting of 25 qualified drivers and 28 qualified firemen, the balance being unqualified, chiefly volunteers. The opportunities for employing 'traffic' volunteers, he contended, were severely restricted whilst the number of trains were so restricted by lack of qualified drivers.

Sunday 9th May

A relief station master, formerly a signalman, refused to take duty at Dr Days signal box and was therefore regarded as a striker. This man was not allowed to resume until 19th June, having been treated identically to the man at Severn Beach. One man went on strike for the second time and five others returned to work; 2,446 were still on strike. By now 274 volunteers were registered, of whom 48 were at work.

Shunting engines were employed at Chippenham, Lawrence Hill, Swindon and Salisbury.

Monday 10th May

A further 18 volunteers had been taken on. Twenty-nine strikers had returned to work yesterday, the total on strike being 2,458, the increase being accounted for by the inclusion of those on annual leave, ill etc. as 'strikers'.

Of the 370 engines normally required each day, only 42 were available, at Bristol (16), Westbury (8), Swindon (9), Weston (2), Yatton (2), and 1 each at Salisbury, Weymouth, Wells, Chippenham and Bridport.

Passenger revenue had gradually been increasing at Temple Meads from £91 on 6th May, £199 on 7th May, £271 on 8th & 9th May (combined) to £244 on 10th May.

A complaint had been received from the Bristol Tramways Co. at the GWR's action in putting on a road service between Chepstow and Monmouth when the Bristol company was 'already maintaining an ample service.'

Tuesday 11th May

The number of engines available increased by three, an extra engine at Bristol and Westbury and a single engine at Frome. Messrs Petter of Yeovil had offered their shunting engine at Yeovil (Hendford), and this was being considered.

Bristol Chamber of Commerce wondered why more freight trains were not being run, but as the superintendent had explained, it was not easy to run a freight train without a qualified driver. A further eight volunteers had been taken on and 25 strikers returned to duty; the number on strike was now 2,436. Passenger receipts at Bristol totalled £201 for the day.

Stones had been thrown at the 11.30 am Bristol to Cardiff at Dr Days bridge, and a non-striking porter at Trowbridge had been molested by a porter colleague who was on strike.

The superintendent and staff had been making visits throughout the division in order to ascertain the true position 'on the ground' and endeavour to raise morale. The position was summarised as 'gradually improving'.

Wednesday 12th May

This was the day that the General Strike was called off at noon, but, as was happening elsewhere on the GWR, the men refused to accept the 're-engagement notification' (circular 3002) and no general return to work took place. There was very little new for the superintendent to report: a few more volunteers taken on, passenger receipts slightly increasing and 27 staff had returned to work. The number still on strike was 2,409. Nine shunting engines had been at work and 22 freight trains (through or local) had worked in the division.

Thursday 13th May

Only seven short branch lines, 'the least important in the division', remained without a train service (*see Chapter Six for details*). Ten shunting engines were at work and 27 freight trains were run. It was anticipated that a total of 53 engines would be available on Friday 14th.

Staff still on strike remained high, 2,359 or 71 per cent of those employed in the division.

Friday 14th May

On this day the railway settlement was made, details being received at Bristol at 6 pm, and this is the last of Mr Griffiths' reports. At 9 pm there were still 2,310 staff on strike; a final total of 93 volunteers were working out of a total of 594 enrolled.*

It was agreed that lists would be prepared of staff in each grade in order of seniority at each location, and that 'the persons [listed] would be sent for to come on duty in turn, according to the order on those lists . . .'

****

This diary makes it clear that much of what has been written about the importance of volunteers has been exaggerated. Without qualified drivers to drive the locomotives, trains could not be run. Without trains there was little need for other staff, apart from those unloading and delivering the goods already in transit when the Strike started, or tending the company's horses.

Included with this diary are some papers which detail the actions taken against this division's traffic personnel dealt with under clauses 4 or 5 of the Strike settlement (*see Chapter Eight*). The station masters at Corsham and Severn

*Presumably only 'traffic' department staff because Appendix Five shows much higher figures for volunteers.

Beach, and the relief station master at Bristol have already been mentioned. The station master at Uffington was moved to the position of goods clerk at Calne (a clause 4 case), although the document is marked 'ultimately removed to Puxton as SM'. (In September 1926 the *GWR Magazine* records the appointment of the SM at Puxton & Worle to Uffington.) An inspector at Bristol was moved to the post of yard inspector at Swindon.

Two signalmen were dealt with under clause 5 of the settlement. A 42 year old signalman (with 20 years service) at Highbridge East went on strike on the first day. He was advised by his station master to return to duty at 2 pm on 17th May, but, following two complaints of intimidation against him, that instruction was withdrawn and the man remained unemployed. He was accused of making rude and menacing remarks to the goods clerk on 11th May and insulting a porter-signalman on 15th May. He was allowed to resume on 12th June, and, eventually, the General Manager agreed to pay him a £10 gratuity in lieu of lost wages as the charges against him were 'somewhat thin'.

A more serious case, and the only case in the Bristol division which culminated in a man's dismissal involved a 36 year old signalman at Dorchester Jn with 17 years' service. At 6.45 pm on 3rd May, the evening before the Strike, this man had entered Dorchester Jn signal box, although not booked on duty until 10 pm, and behaved 'in an insulting and menacing manner' to the signalman on duty. He was told to leave, but when he returned at 10 pm, 'he allowed a number of unauthorised persons to enter the box to carry on the discussions there.' He was dismissed on 11th June and the sentence was confirmed on 23rd June. Mr Griffiths notes: 'This case has been more than once discussed with the superintendent of the line who has stated in emphatic terms that . . . no less punishment than dismissal is called for.' The General Manager heard a second appeal on 19th November, but with a comment like that on record the outcome was fairly obvious. The appeal was rejected, although the company agreed to assist in finding the man a new job (but not on the GWR).

One wonders why the station master at such a rural station as this should have gone on strike. This is Uffington, junction for Faringdon, looking towards London. The station master was in class 4 and had a staff of 7, none of them clerical staff. In 1926 paybill costs were £1,351 and receipts £7,511. *British Rail*

GWR shareholder Mr Francis Roxburgh acting as a volunteer porter at Paddington; he probably did not get too involved with the fish in that clothing! *Railway Gazette*

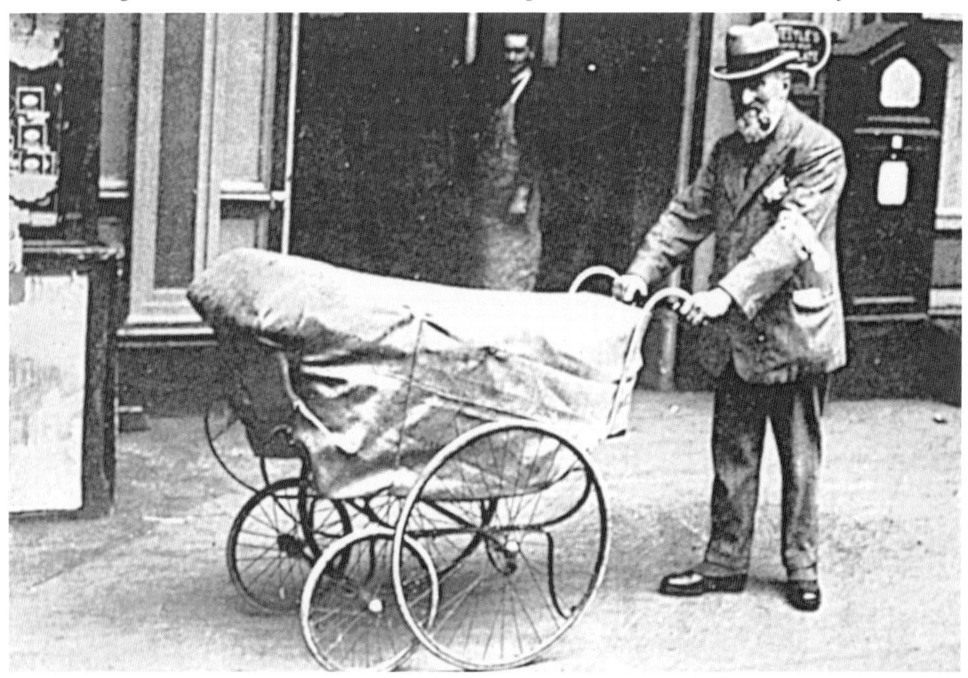

Chapter Five

The Volunteers

Building upon experience gained in the 1919 railwaymen's strike, the GWR quickly instituted arrangements whereby volunteers for railway work could be interviewed and allocated suitable work, if found satisfactory. At Paddington, and 11 other main centres, recruiting centres were set up and provision made to select volunteers to fill posts in the following groups of jobs:

engine drivers, firemen, mechanics and shed labourers
motor drivers and mechanics
horse drivers and stablemen
electrical and signal & telegraph engineers
guards, shunters, signalmen, ticket collectors and porters
goods porters
police
maintenance labourers (presumably permanent way?)

A colour card system was employed depending on the background of the volunteer, as follows:

white - male volunteers, non GWR employees
yellow - GW staff volunteers
pink - retired GW staff volunteers
green - women and clerks

At Paddington the General Meeting Room in the headquarters' offices was used as a recruiting centre. Little activity took place on the first day before the Strike, 3rd May, but on Tuesday 4th May 'the number of volunteers grew rapidly - more rapidly than the demand.' Nearly all the volunteers were unskilled in railway work, but the GWR official report on the Volunteer Organisation notes that they had 'an excellent supply of men - from the Hospitals, Universities and Public Schools - of good education and physique, and eager to perform any kind of useful work'.

By Tuesday night, with the Volunteer Office filled with unplaced volunteers, it became obvious that the staffing of Paddington station was inadequate and that there was plenty of work for volunteers. The report notes that Paddington station did not seem able to anticipate the possible demand for labour, and, each day, the Volunteer Office formed up gangs ready for duty that night, and each day *their* anticipation proved correct and the group was sent to the station. Eventually the Volunteer Office took over the whole of the arrangements for supply of volunteer labour to Paddington station, including provision of foremen, timekeepers etc. for volunteers. Thus arose the unique situation that the equivalent of the General Manager's office was directing staff at Paddington station, an activity normally controlled three tiers below (supt of the line, divisional supt, station master). This, it is noted, 'was outside the remit of the Volunteer Office but it is considered

Volunteers unloading food baskets at Paddington. *Railway Gazette*

Several photographs were taken of the lady volunteers employed in the stables at Paddington; here Miss J. Williams poses with one of her charges, 11th May, 1926. *Railway Gazette*

In this picture Miss Austin and Mrs Davies are seen exercising horses at Paddington stables on 11th May, 1926. *Hulton Deutsch Collection Ltd*

This scene shows that gentlemen volunteers were also involved in looking after the horses at Paddington stables. *Courtesy GWR Museum, Swindon*

A final look at Paddington stables; here the Hon. Mrs Beaumont and Miss Coventry are grooming the horses (11th May, 1926). *Hulton Deutsch Collection Ltd*

Volunteers load eggs for deliveries from Paddington. The headgear probably gives a clue to the normal occupations of the wearers. *Great Western Trust*

the expedient was justified by the results . . .'

Enrolment of volunteers 'proceeded at high pressure during Wednesday and the succeeding days and men with experience were placed rapidly'. Amongst activities covered were a party of men and women for stabling duties in London (*see photographs*), a special coaling gang at Old Oak Common, men and women placed as lorry drivers, an emergency gang for unexpected engineering work, and suitable men were passed to the Police department for use as special constables. Three doctors from St Mary's Hospital, Paddington manned a First Aid post on No. 1 platform.

A simplified course of instruction for signalmen was drawn up by Mr E.S. Hadley, the editor of the *GWR Magazine*, and training was carried out at Royal Oak signalling school. The first page of the signalmen's course is included as an illustration. No less than 252 men were trained at Royal Oak, of which 231 were utilised throughout the system. The company was afterwards complimented upon the 'lucidity and completeness' of the instructions used 'by experienced lecturers from the universities'. Similar arrangements were made for trainee guards and shunters (see illustration of excerpt from their training instructions), and this included practical training in Paddington Yard.

Appendix Five shows the total number of volunteers enrolled at Paddington, and at the other 11 enrolment centres. Whilst the Paddington figures are broken down into the various grades of staff, the provincial centres only record total numbers. Note that at Paddington only 40 per cent of those enrolled were actually used; the equivalent figure taken from the totals column of the 11 provincial centres is 43 per cent. A separate table shows the number of volunteer drivers and firemen trained in the nine Motive Power department divisions. Of the 219 men trained at Old Oak Common, 47 were sent to other depots for employment.

In summarising the 'Lessons Learned' the report (RAIL 253/451, PRO Kew) notes that, in the event of a future similar event, and to overcome the problems experienced of lack of anticipation of labour requirements, each station or depot should set up a skeleton organisation. 'Even if the staff is a little in excess of immediate needs, there is the great advantage that the new men are obtaining experience instead of having to learn their duties when the expansion actually takes place'.

The other 'lesson' specifically noted is that trained signalmen had been kept waiting orders for days in London, and then suddenly sent for. Whereas if they had been 'distributed', they could have learned their boxes in readiness to take over as the train service grew. This had caused some discontent amongst eager volunteers who were kept waiting about, having been passed out at Royal Oak.

From time to time while researching the General Strike, I have come across statements of damage caused to equipment, principally locomotives, by volunteers. Confirmation is not, however, given of this in official documents. Possibly if damage was caused, it was hushed up. R.S. Joby in his book *The Railwaymen* has this to say:

> A fair amount of damage was caused by the unskilled driving and firing: fireboxes full of fused clinker, firetubes wedged with lumps of coke and hot axleboxes, were but a few

CHAPTER II.

SIGNALS AND THEIR USES.

IMAGINE yourself the engine-driver of a non-stop train travelling at a-mile-a-minute. For an hour or so you have rushed along and passed any number of stations where all the signals were showing "All Right," and you anticipated nothing to check your rapid progress. If, suddenly, you came to a signal showing "Stop," what would happen? With the weight of a heavy train behind the engine, you would be unable to obey the signal before you had gone a long way past it. Besides, the abrupt stoppage of a fast-travelling train would throw the passengers from their seats, jerk the luggage off the carriage racks upon their heads, and do no end of other mischief. Obviously, the system of signalling has had to be arranged in a way that prevents such an occurrence.

The situation is met in a simple manner. Whenever an engine-driver is required to stop his train at a signal, he is given warning *a long way distant*, so as to allow him ample time to reduce the speed of the train before reaching the signal.

Distant Signals.

The first of your signals seen by the engine-driver of a train approaching you from either direction, is a considerable way distant from your signal box. Its position gives it the name of "**Distant**" signal. Between this signal and the next one will be a distance of, perhaps, 1,000 yards or so.

Now, whenever an engine-driver sees a **Distant** signal at "**Danger**" he is not expected to stop at it, but to regard it as a **Caution Signal**, indicating that he must reduce the speed of his train and be prepared to stop at the next signal, if it should be at "**Danger.**"

The arm of a Distant signal has a peculiar shape, being notched at the end. See illustrations on the next page.

Home and Starting Signals.

The second signal reached by an approaching train is generally situated in the neighbourhood of the signal box. Its position gives it the name of the "**Home**" signal. It is a **Stop** signal, and must not be passed at "**Danger.**" The **Home** signal is usually placed a few yards short of the first siding connection or other points on the line to which the signal applies. This enables an approaching train to be stopped where it will stand clear of any shunting or other operations to be done over the points. At junctions the Home signals are placed where, in a similar way, they "protect" the lines which other trains may require to pass over. See diagrams on pages 17 and 18.

Farther on, ahead of the station platform and points of any sidings worked from the signal box, and generally some little distance beyond the signal box itself, is another signal. Its purpose is to govern the *starting away of trains* from your control into the section in advance. The name given it, therefore, is the "**Starting**" signal.

When the Starting signal is at Danger, the Home signal must not be lowered for an approaching train until the train is close to the Home signal

A page from the simplified instructions issued to volunteer signalmen.

RAILWAY SHUNTING

FREIGHT TRAIN VEHICLES

PRACTICAL OPERATIONS

The example given in the first illustration shows in a simple manner how railway shunting work is done :—

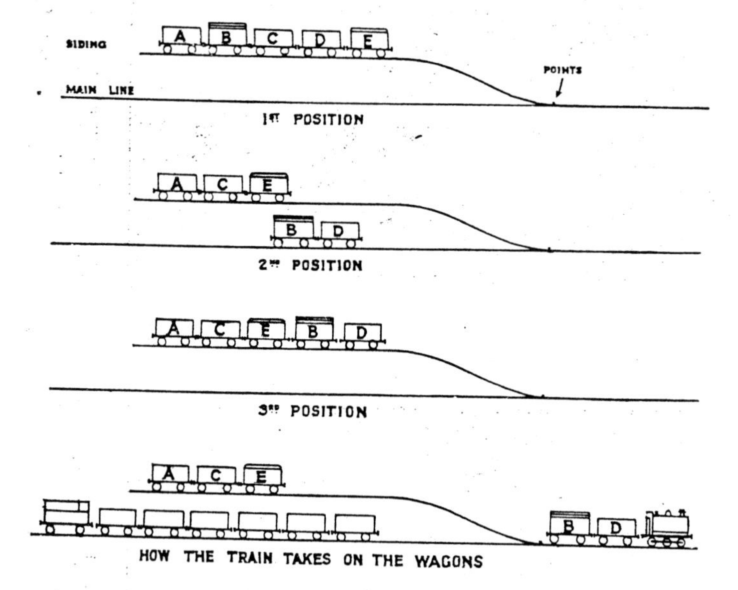

Here are five trucks (lettered A to E) on a siding. Suppose you require to place the two marked " B " and " D " into a position to be taken on by a train which, later, will arrive on the main line. This is how you proceed :—

Join the engine to truck " E," see that " B " " C " " D " and " E " are coupled together, and that " B " is detached from " A." Draw forward the four trucks that are connected together. When " B " has passed over the points, detach " B " and push it on to the main line. Again reverse the points, and push " C " on to the siding. In like manner shunt " D " on to the main line, and " E " on to the siding. Detach the engine from " E " and attach it to the two trucks (" B " and " D ") on the main line. Then place these trucks on the siding. They will therefore stand at the " points " or " outlet " end of the other wagons.

When the train arrives on the main line, it must come to a stand a little distance short of the points. Its engine must be detached and sent into the siding to " pick up " " B " and " D." It must then push these wagons against the train on the main line. Then join the connecting (" coupling ") chains, and the train will be ready to proceed.

A page from the instructions issued to volunteer shunters.

of the maladies which had to be repaired afterwards. On the minimal one day's training received by signalmen it was as well that traffic was very light.

And in Jeffery Skelley's book *The General Strike 1926* Angela Tuckett in a chapter on Swindon says,

. . . the inexperienced volunteers on the footplate did massive damage. It was estimated that it took two years to repair all the damage caused during those days by ignorant or inexperienced volunteers.

Angela Tuckett wrote of a volunteer fireman who, ten years earlier, had been a cleaner at Swindon, but had left Swindon after being involved in a fight at work. Recently returned to Swindon, he was seen by the shed foreman and offered a permanent job if he would fire to a volunteer driver. However, when the strike ended all he received was a certificate and a postal order for 21*s*.!

A trick employed by strikers was to grease the rails on inclines - this made the engine wheels slip and the 'inexperienced firemen sweat'. Angela Tuckett also describes a 'gentleman volunteer' temporary footplateman who could not stop his train at Bristol Temple Meads and only succeeded in pulling up near Bath by emptying the firebox (one feels that this story may have been exaggerated in its telling and retelling over the years!). At Chippenham the station master was assisted by a local tradesman as ticket collector, a local landowner as porter and a political agent as booking clerk! Apparently the local trades unionists were not too upset as they considered the temporary staff less than competent.

The best volunteer's account found by the author is that by C.R. Clinker who was then a clerk in the Bristol divisional superintendent's office. He volunteered to work as a signalman and an abbreviated version of his account (now held at Brunel University) is as follows. Unfortunately he does not identify any of the locations worked at, although the first location is Codford (*see Chapter Four*).

It would be wrong to give the impression that the General Strike was anything but a very serious calamity. Yet to a young man in his twenties, with only three years service, it provided an interlude in daily routine and a sense of excitement.

Monday morning's work in the office was much as usual. But after lunch all suddenly became tense. The staff was handed copies of a telegram from the General Manager urging each 'Great Western man' to hesitate before breaking his contract of service with 'the old company'. At four we were summoned to the Board Room - the only occasion I remember seeing all the staff assembled together. We were asked to indicate on a list whether we intended to remain at work and, if we did so, what we would undertake. It was an awesome decision. Having recently passed my Signalling exam. with 85 per cent marks I signed up for 'any work', with no clear idea of what this might involve. We were told to go home and report for duty at 6 am.

Being unable to sleep, I got up early, put a few necessaries in a small bag and walked the 2½ miles to the station, arriving there about 4.30 am. The scene at Temple Meads was quite extraordinary. Every platform was blocked by trains without engines. The enginemen had just detached their engines on arrival and gone to shed. In No. 4 (the up main platform) stood the Penzance-Paddington Postal from which the Post Office had removed their bags. Several of the station inspectors were about, few of the supervisory staff having joined the Strike. The refreshment rooms opened at 6 am as usual and promised a welcome meeting place.

At the office, it appeared that only four of the staff had elected to strike, but only three of the loyal men were prepared to take on anything.

News came in that two of the station masters had struck. One, on the main line had foolishly instructed his signalman to leave the level crossing gates across the line, contrary to standing instructions. The other, on a very rural double line branch in Wiltshire, had done the same at two crossings under his supervision. I was sent to the latter [Codford] in the office car and dumped seemingly in the middle of nowhere.

Having obtained the keys of the station from the station master and locked up, I walked up the road to the village to find some lodgings for a night or two. I was kindly received at the little hotel, to whom I explained that my meal times might be irregular, and so on.

Back at the station I telephoned up and down the line to see if any train was about, but there was no news. A farmer arrived with a dozen milk churns. I had no idea of how to charge or invoice milk. We did not deal with such traffic at the station where I had been trained. I accepted it, wrote out a waybill marked 'charges to follow' and left the load for the first train that might appear.

Towards midday the station master's wife spoke to me over the hedge separating the garden from the platform. She said her husband had gone out and would I like some lunch on a tray? I accepted and this surreptitious arrangement was continued several times a day while I remained there. An odd arrangement to be fed by a station master's wife!

Just as I was sitting down to my first lunch, a train arrived unheralded. Block working was suspended and it had come up the line ignoring signals. It was manned by a retired driver and his very juvenile son as fireman; the guard was a regular man. I unlocked the gates, passed the train through and rode with it for about half a mile to the second crossing. Here I encountered the crossing keeper's wife, a foul-mouthed unpleasant woman who shouted abuse at me whilst I handled the gates. The train went on its way and I returned on foot to my lunch.

After four days in this delightfully rural spot, a telephone message told me that one of our relief station masters was on the way to take over, and that I was to go to a small junction signal box on the main line.

This promised to be more interesting and would not have been over arduous had not the station master been thoroughly objectionable and unhelpful. To be pitched into a strange signal box, albeit of only 18 levers, and expected to commence work at once without time to examine the diagram or grasp the locking, was difficult enough. It was much more difficult trying to get my bearings amid an almost ceaseless string of invective. I devoutly wished the station master had gone on strike.

Fortunately after two days and a night in which time I had passed some 40 trains, I was able to move on, this time to a large junction box in Bristol where I joined an office colleague older than myself. The disadvantage of its situation was proximity to a public road overbridge from which vantage point men, and some women, had been throwing stones and other missiles on to the lines and at the box windows. Half the glass had gone when I arrived and nearly all was shattered before we were withdrawn on termination of the strike three days later. The electric batteries were exhausted and we were without block instruments or telephones. All we could do was to work such mechanical levers as were not electrically locked.

After six days and nights without sleep I was in a daze without any sort of feeling left in me except an overwhelming desire to go to bed. I took a taxi to my lodging, refused any food and could hardly keep awake whilst I undressed and flopped into bed. But I was too tired for immediate sleep and it was several hours before I got off. I awoke two days later.

Volunteers unloading parcels at Swindon Town station, 14th May, 1926.

Hulton Deutsch Collection Ltd

Ealing Broadway signal box, which was worked in the Strike by Mr S.G. Hearn, then a GWR special trainee, who later rose to be the second Western Region chief operating superintendent on the retirement of Gilbert Matthews, the former (and last) GWR superintendent of the line. Ealing was a special class signal box with a 39 lever frame, seen here, it is thought , in 1938. The box closed in March 1955 when West Ealing's area of control was expanded.

British Rail, courtesy J.P. Morris

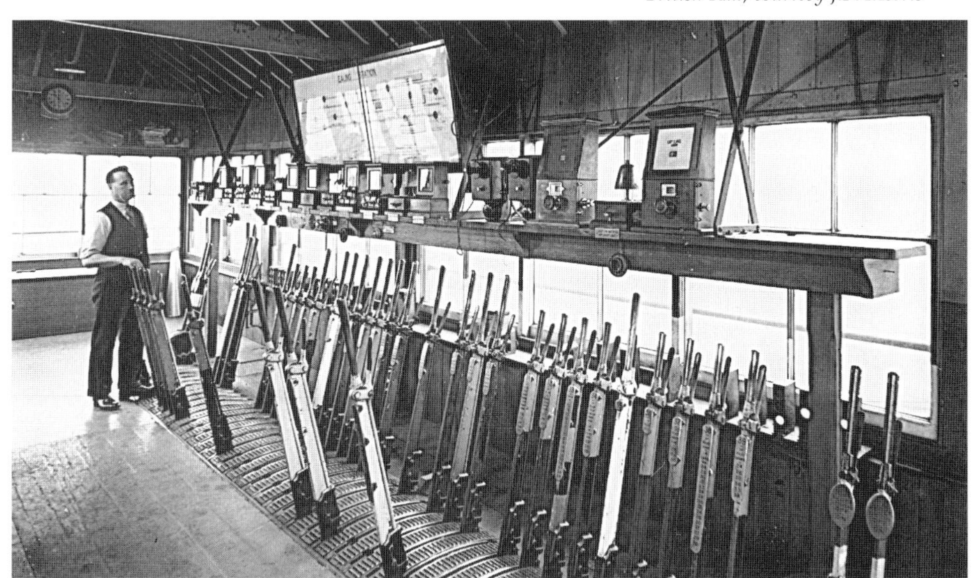

It was a great relief to be told that I might take two weeks special leave. This I spent at home in the Midlands and returned to normal life at the office fully refreshed.

Restoration of the havoc caused by the Strike was a protracted business. On the goods side movement had been virtually suspended except for foodstuffs, petrol and other necessaries. Traders had used road transport and continued to do so in some cases. Much valuable traffic was permanently lost to the railways and a good deal that resumed did so only slowly.

In the traffic department, passenger trains were very gradually restored, coach and engine workings were extracted from the muddle into which hand-to-mouth working had driven them. Signalling equipment was overhauled and set to rights. It was officially stated that full normal working was not restored until the summer of 1927.

I do not know how the membership of trade unions among GW staff compared with those of other companies at this time. At a number of places in the Division there were certainly strong trade union branches, notably at Swindon, Trowbridge, Westbury and Bristol. At smaller places the interest seemed lukewarm.

The Railway Clerks' Association did not appear to attract many members of the divisional office staff. I doubt if more than 15 per cent belonged to it. So far as I could see, the interest in union activities was negligible - virtually non existent. My membership was never canvassed during the whole of my service with the Company.

S.G. Hearn, who at that time was a GWR 'special trainee', and later rose to be the second Western Region chief operating superintendent following the retirement of Gilbert Matthews, volunteered to work Ealing Broadway signal box:

The hours were long . . . although the trains were few to start with. I would open about 6 am and on one or two occasions did not finish until 2 am the next day. This was due to several 'banana specials' from Avonmouth Docks which arrived up late at night. Someone reported that they did not think that it was right for a signalman to work such long hours . . . and the chief clerk of the SOL office came out to visit me and I soon satisfied him there was no cause for alarm.

Mr Hearn records that his wife and young son used to bring food to the box each day; his son used to climb on chairs to ring the bells and took a delight in pushing the lever dusters down through gaps in the lever frame!

Another GWR special trainee who worked as a signalman was Arthur (later Sir Arthur) Kirby who volunteered to work the very large signal box at Reading East Main. Unfortunately for him, his father was district inspector at Reading and would have none of it. He told his son that he had never had a serious train crash in his district and did not intend to have one now! Arthur Kirby was sent to Southcote Jn which he worked throughout the Strike without 'any untoward incident'. Later Arthur Kirby left the GWR, spending many years managing African railways, later becoming involved in politics there and diplomacy in London, then becoming chairman of the British Transport Docks Board and finally the chairman of the National Ports Council. A varied life indeed!

The *Newbury Weekly News* recorded that no goods trains ran below Hungerford during the Strike 'until yesterday [12th May] when volunteers ran one from Newbury to Westbury, making a wonderful run, and returning with the engine. At both Didcot and Reading yesterday, the numbers of volunteer drivers and firemen were in excess of the engines available.'

The 'official' caption to this picture reads: 'Lord Portarlington superintending the unloading of fish at Paddington', but I suspect the gentlemen in overalls could manage quite nicely, thank you, without 'superintendence'! *Hulton Deutsch Collection Ltd*

The now famous picture of volunteer lorry driver Mrs Talbot at Paddington station. Notice the barbed wire on the bonnet; according to a report written after the Strike, Mrs Talbot had her vehicle 'stormed by the mob' (*see Chapter 7*). *Hulton Deutsch Collection Ltd*

Mr James Page, formerly the station master at Paddington, then retired and acting as a guard on the GWR's Barnstaple branch during the Strike. *Railway Gazette*

A leaflet entitled 'How the "Gentlemen of England" Man the Trains', published during the Strike by the TUC, is scathing indeed about the volunteers:

> THE GOVERNMENT TRIES TO PERSUADE YOU THAT BUSINESS IS AS USUAL
>
> The truth is that transport and productive industry are practically at a standstill.
>
> Do you realise the work of the railway services of Great Britain?
>
> In 1924, the total mileage of journeys and shunting was over 580 millions; that is, more than one and a half millions a day.
>
> The number of passengers was 1,236,000,000 or over three and a third millions a day.
>
> The railways carry merchandise, coal and minerals amounting to 1,100,000 tons per day, and 67,000 tons of livestock. Practically the whole of this work has been stopped.
>
> The Government issue bulletins saying that the railway services are improving day by day.
>
> What does this improvement amount to? They boasted of 200 trains a day on the Southern Railway on Thursday but from the two big railway stations, Victoria and Waterloo alone, the number is normally 1,880.
>
> At Victoria today (Saturday) the Company 'hopes' to run 20 trains.
>
> The whole North Eastern Railway claimed to run 500 on Thursday. Newcastle Central has normally 954 trains per day. From two of the big London stations on this system the usual number is over 1,500 and the mileage on that railway averages half a million miles a day.
>
> How can the feeble little army of blacklegs deal with such a task as this?
>
> Compare your broadcasting programme with these facts.

In his memoirs, *Felix Pole, His Book*, Sir Felix Pole, the General Manager of the GWR says that at the first Board meeting after the Strike he was asked how many of the volunteers would be retained in permanent posts. He pointed out that the terms of the settlement required that the regular staff should be taken back as and when work was available, and that no volunteers would therefore be employed.

There was some criticism of this by the Directors, but after Sir Felix had said that the vast majority of volunteers had returned to their regular work, and of those remaining some would be men previously dismissed, or undesirable for some other reason, the matter was not pursued.

In his book Sir Felix relates an amusing story of how the Secretary of the Paddington Volunteers Committee had 'done a bunk' with money set aside for a volunteers' reunion dinner, causing the company to have to underwrite the cost of the dinner:

> Shortly after the Strike I received a letter from [the Secretary] to the effect that the Committee had been considering the future; that they felt strongly that the volunteer organisation should be kept in being . . . and that they had come to the conclusion that the best thing was to have an annual dinner of Great Western Volunteers. The first dinner was to take place in the Piccadilly Hotel and an invitation was extended to me . . . The great evening arrived and the Secretary of the Committee was there dressed in a smart and obviously new dinner jacket, while the guests included Lord Churchill, Sir Ernest Palmer, Colonel Churchill, Lord Macmillan . . . and many others, more especially (be it noted) three of the 'big five' Scotland Yard detectives. The various volunteers wore emblems of their work. Engine drivers and firemen in dungarees, policemen with

truncheons; volunteer ticket collectors snipped the tickets of all the visitors. The dinner was good . . . and all the guests voted the evening a huge success.

The next morning the Secretary of the Volunteer Committee wrote to all the prominent visitors expressing the Committee's delight at the success of the evening. To this he added a statement that unfortunately the cost of the dinner had been underestimated . . . [and that] some of the guests might like to contribute. A large number of cheques resulted. Shortly after, a cheque drawn by the Volunteer's Committee secretary and cashed in the Hotel came back marked 'R.D.' The Company's Secretary, Mr Davies, sent for the Volunteer's Secretary who said: 'How stupid of me. I have two banking accounts and have drawn on the wrong one. I will give you another cheque.' Alas, this also came back 'R.D.' and this time the drawer was not so confident and, shortly after, it was learnt that the Committee had been dissolved. . . Mr Davies became a little suspicious and enquired whether the dinner had been paid for. He found it had not and that the Volunteers' Committee Secretary had decamped with all the money paid for tickets, plus the cheques sent in by enthusiastic guests.

On enquiry at Scotland Yard the erstwhile secretary was identified and it transpired that he had just been released from prison after serving a sentence of three years. His misapplied ability had deceived many . . . Naturally, the whole matter had to be kept secret but the dinner cost the Company some hundreds of pounds.

Most volunteers had been unpaid and after the Strike all of these volunteers were given a present by the company, accompanied by a card expressing the company's grateful thanks for services rendered, *see illustration*. In his book Sir Felix records that he had intended the present to be a piece of Worcester china.

I was in favour of a nice piece of Worcester china, on which could be reproduced in colour a photograph showing how active Paddington station was during the strike. Unfortunately, the Worcester china people could not undertake what would have been for them a very large order. The final decision was that the volunteers and staff who had assisted should be given a silver ashtray inscribed: 'General Strike, May, 1926. With grateful thanks of the Great Western Railway Company.'

After the Strike, staff newly appointed to the supervisory grades were required to sign an undertaking not to withdraw their labour except by giving the requisite notice. These same forms were still being used in the 1960s - *see illustration on page 102*.

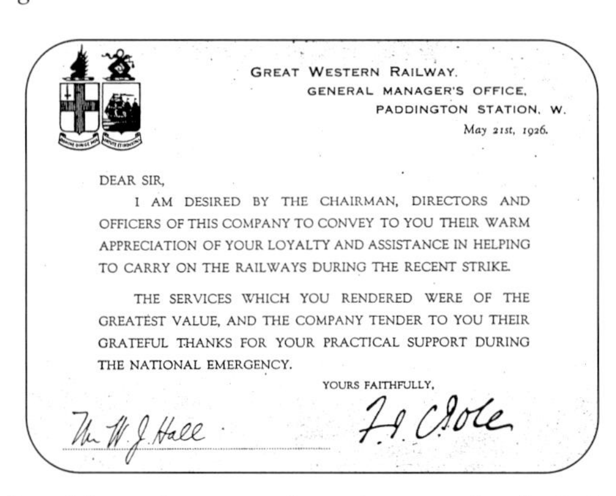

GREAT WESTERN RAILWAY.
GENERAL MANAGER'S OFFICE,
PADDINGTON STATION, W.
May 21st, 1926.

DEAR SIR,

I AM DESIRED BY THE CHAIRMAN, DIRECTORS AND OFFICERS OF THIS COMPANY TO CONVEY TO YOU THEIR WARM APPRECIATION OF YOUR LOYALTY AND ASSISTANCE IN HELPING TO CARRY ON THE RAILWAYS DURING THE RECENT STRIKE.

THE SERVICES WHICH YOU RENDERED WERE OF THE GREATEST VALUE, AND THE COMPANY TENDER TO YOU THEIR GRATEFUL THANKS FOR YOUR PRACTICAL SUPPORT DURING THE NATIONAL EMERGENCY.

YOURS FAITHFULLY,

Mr W. J. Hall

F. J. C. Pole

One of the cards presented to volunteers after the Strike.

Chapter Six

Bristol Division Train Services

There is a comprehensive collection of daily train notices for the Bristol division during the Strike period, preserved by Mr C.R. Clinker, and now held at Brunel University, Uxbridge. I thought it would give a flavour of living through this now far-off event to devote a chapter to some of the Strike history recorded in these notices. Where reference is made to variations from the plan, this has been established from the minutes of the daily Chief Officers' Conference (file RAIL250/748 at PRO, Kew).

The first notice in the collection is for *Wednesday 5th May* and shows a special service of 10 up and 9 down trains between Weston-super-Mare and Bristol (Temple Meads) from 8.30 am to 8.45 pm, plus one each way between Yatton and Bristol. The service is split between two train sets, one of which is the Clevedon branch auto-train. All up trains are required to run via the Bristol Avoiding line from Bristol West to North Somerset Jn, thence into Temple Meads (TM), which would avoid any shunting movements at TM by turning the train for its return journey westwards.

Other services planned are two trips Wells-Bristol and back (up trains again running via the Bristol Avoiding line), and four trains in each direction between Bristol and Trowbridge, two of which are extended to and from Salisbury. All the trains so far referred to call at all intermediate stations. (In fact a few additional services ran, mainly between Swindon and Bristol and Bristol and Cardiff.)

The only other trains shown in the Bristol division notice for 5th May are a 9.15 am Paddington-Plymouth via Bristol, 10.30 am Bristol-Paddington [this left 61 minutes late with about 100 passengers], 11.55 am Paddington-Cardiff via Gloucester and 12.30 pm milk empties Paddington-Frome via Chippenham and Melksham. In the event a 2.30 pm and 5.35 pm Bristol-Paddington and 6.30 pm Paddington-Bristol also ran, as well as an 8.55 am Weymouth-Paddington.

Thursday 6th May shows a marked improvement. The Weston-super-Mare and Wells services are unchanged. The Salisbury timetable is improved by extra trains between Bristol and Bath only, although there is one less train to/from Trowbridge. The services to Salisbury are speeded up to call at less intermediate stations and one each way is extended to/from Cardiff. There are a further two trains each way to/from Cardiff. A new service is planned between Weymouth and Westbury with two up and one down trains calling at all stations. Although not shown on the notice, the Avonmouth branch reopened with four trains each way between Bristol and Avonmouth.

On the main line there are two trains from Bristol to Paddington at 9.35 am and 11.15 am and a third at 3.0 pm (9.25 am from Plymouth). The London down trains are not listed but the Chief Officers' Conference minutes show that trains left Paddington at 9.15 am (Bristol TM), 11.55 am (Cardiff), 2.0 pm (Plymouth via Bristol), 4.30 pm (Weymouth) and 6.30 pm (Bristol TM). There are two trains from Bristol to the West Country, a 10.45 am to Newton Abbot (worked by a Newton Abbot engine) and a 1.45 pm to Exeter (worked by a Bristol engine).

The Weston, Wells, Salisbury, Cardiff and Weymouth services operated in the same way on *Friday 7th May*. New services started up were four trains from Swindon to Gloucester (two extended to Cardiff) and one Cardiff-Swindon via Gloucester, one Cardiff to Gloucester and three Gloucester-Swindon workings.

On the main line there were two up trains from TM to Paddington at 9.35 am and 3.15 pm (9.35 am ex-Plymouth), a 9.30 am Swindon-Paddington, and three planned trains from Bristol (Stapleton Rd) to Paddington at 11.15 am, 1.15 and 4.15 pm: these trains had started their journeys at Cardiff. After calling at Lawrence Hill they ran direct to Bath avoiding Temple Meads. In the down direction services were similar to Thursday; additionally an 11.45 am Weymouth-Paddington and a 10.10 am milk empties Paddington-Weymouth ran. The service previously recorded between Bristol-Newton Abbot/Exeter again ran, except that there was also a 4.30 pm Newton Abbot-Bristol return service.

For some reason there are no notices for *Saturday 8th May* in the Clinker Collection, but the daily GWR conference already mentioned appended a list of trains run up to 9.0 pm the previous day. (This was the last day for which the minutes listed individual trains - hereafter only summary totals are given.) From this it can be established that Saturday's services were similar to Friday's, with the addition of a 3.55 pm Bristol-Plymouth. The Clevedon branch reopened with five return trips, as did the Portishead branch with an 8.45 am Bristol-Portishead. This was followed by three return shuttles between Portishead and Clifton Bridge, then a 6.30 pm Portishead-Bristol. The first mention of a train over the former Midland & South Western Junction (M&SWJ) is to be found with a 10.28 am Cheltenham Lansdown-Swindon Town and a 4.0 pm return journey.

The service for *Sunday 9th May* bears a great similarity to those on preceding days and one feels that it was considered important to run as many trains as possible, even if the service provided was more generous that for a normal Sunday. For example the Clevedon branch boasts six return trips, there are four to Avonmouth Dock and back and even one return journey from Wells (although this was probably run for the milk traffic). Main line and cross-country trains are much the same as for Saturday, including the solitary one each way on the M&SWJ line.

By *Monday 10th May* the main line service appears to have become fairly settled to the pattern of the previous days and any expansion is to be found on the branch lines. But there is the first mention of a train from Penzance calling in the Bristol Division, a 9.0 am 'perishables' Penzance to Paddington 'calling as ordered'. A new rail motor service from Weymouth to Dorchester promised four return trips and, for the first time, four SR trains to/from Weymouth are included, all calling at Upwey Junction. Interestingly, two are booked to leave Weymouth at the same time as the 3.30 pm and 5.45 pm Weymouth-Dorchester railmotors, suggesting that the SR and GWR Timebill clerks had not got their heads together! The Clevedon branch is now boosted to 10 return trips, the first leaving Yatton at 7.50 am and the last leaving Clevedon at 6.45 pm. The

Avonmouth Dock service is increased to hourly with clock face departures from Bristol between 9.15 am and 6.15 pm. There is an extra shuttle between Portishead and Clifton Bridge (making four), and, for the first time, a service is shown on the Calne branch: two goods and one passenger (down) and three passenger trains (up). (The branch had reopened to 'freight only' the previous day.)

On *Tuesday 11th May* the 9.0 am 'perishable' Penzance to Paddington is shown to convey passengers from Bristol onwards, leaving that place at 'about 7.0 pm', thus giving a later departure to the capital. One suspects, however, that only those really desperate to reach London would have waited for this rather uncertain departure time. The 2.0 pm Paddington-Plymouth (via Bristol) is shown to run only to Newton Abbot, demonstrating how the services could be altered on a daily basis, depending on the availability of manpower. The Bridport branch reopened with a modest three trains in each direction, leaving Bridport at 8.30, 11.30 am and 4.45 pm and Maiden Newton at 10.0 am, 2.0 and 6.0 pm. An extra service on the M&SWJ left Cheltenham at 3.0 pm for Ludgershall, returning therefrom at 5.40 pm. The GWR boat to the Channel Islands 'will sail from Weymouth on Tuesday, Thursday and Saturday as usual.'

On *Wednesday 12th May* things have improved so much that it is possible to run a 12.30 pm Plymouth to Paddington via the Berks & Hants line, including a non-stop run from Taunton to Reading. This must have seemed heavenly to passengers because most trains were calling just about everywhere - Bristol to London trains, for example, were stopping at Bath, Chippenham, Swindon, Didcot, Reading, Maidenhead, Slough, West Drayton and Ealing Broadway. Some services even called at Dauntsey and Wootton Bassett.

The Weymouth-Dorchester shuttle increased by one return trip (to five) and one of the three trains on the Bridport branch was extended to Dorchester. A new appearance on the notice was the North Somerset line with two trains in each direction between Frome and TM via Radstock. The service on the M&SWJ had now returned to one in each direction, but this ran to and from Southampton, leaving Cheltenham at 10.28 am and Southampton at 4.42 pm. A note says that inspector Gilkes of Cheltenham will travel with these trains throughout, and work points at signal boxes between Red Posts Jn and Southampton, as required.

Until now the daily notices had been produced by roneo machine, with very poor quality reproduction. On *Thursday 13th May* a properly printed schedule of Bristol division passenger services was produced, and this is included intact within these pages as it enables the reader to see the full details of everything so far described. New on the scene are services on the Marlborough branch, the Yeovil branch (one train each way), the Portland branch and an apparent extension of the Wells service to Shepton Mallett, although this may have occurred earlier but not been recorded. The 9.0 am Penzance to Paddington, optimistically expected to leave Bristol at 7.0 pm on 11th May, had become 7.30 pm on 12th May and is now 7.50 pm, be it noted.

Readers used, these days, to being whisked between Bristol and London in about 100 minutes will have difficulty understanding how it could take 3½-3¾ hours to cover the same distance.

GREAT WESTERN RAILWAY.

PASSENGER TRAIN SERVICES

BRISTOL DIVISION.

THURSDAY, MAY 13th,

AND UNTIL FURTHER NOTICE.

Other trains will be arranged at short notice as circumstances permit.

FOR SUNDAY SERVICE, SEE SEPARATE NOTICE.

DIDCOT, SWINDON, BATH AND BRISTOL.

		A.M.	A.M.	A.M.	A.M.	A.M.	A.M.	A.M.
Paddington	dep.	..	..	..	8 55	9 15	..	..
Didcot	,,	..	7 43	9 43	10 40	11 0	..	11 15
Steventon	,,	..	7 53	9 53	—	—	..	11 23
Wantage Road	,,	..	8 4	10 4	—	—	..	11 33
Challow	,,	..	8 12	10 12	—	—	..	11 43
Uffington	,,	..	8 20	10 20	—	—	..	11 51
Shrivenham	,,	..	8 30	10 30	—	—	..	12 1
Swindon	arr.	..	8 40	10 40	11 5	11 25	..	12 11
	dep.	..	9 20		11 10	11 30	11 45	
Wootton Bassett	dep.	..	9 35	..	—	—	11 55	..
Dauntsey	,,	..	9 50	..	—	—	12 5	..
Chippenham	,,	8 15	10 5	..	11 35	11 55	12 20	..
Corsham	,,	8 25	10 15	..	—	—	12 30	..
Box	,,	8 33	10 25	..	—	—	12 40	..
Bathampton	,,	8 40	10 33	..	—	—	12 48	..
Bath	,,	8 45	10 40	..	12 0	12 20	12 58	..
Temple Meads	arr.		11 15	..	..	12 40	1 33	..
Stapleton Road	arr.	..	..	..	12 20	..	..	..

		A.M.	P.M.	P.M.	P.M.	P.M.	P.M.	P.M.
Paddington	dep.	11 55	..	..	2 0	..	5 15	6 30
Didcot	,,	2 5	..	..	3 50	..	7 5	8 35
Steventon	,,	—	..	..	—	..	—	—
Wantage Road	,,	—	..	..	—	..	7 20	—
Challow	,,	—	..	..	—	..	7 30	—
Uffington	,,	—	..	..	—	..	7 38	—
Shrivenham	,,	—	..	..	—	..	7 48	—
Swindon	arr.	2 30	..	..	4 15	..	8 0	9 0
	dep.		2 40	2 55	4 25	4 35		9 10
Wootton Bassett	dep.	..	2 50	3 5	—	4 45	..	—
Dauntsey	,,	..	3 0	3 15	—	4 55	..	—
Chippenham	,,	..	3K10	3 30	4 50	5 K5	..	9 40
Corsham	,,	..		3 40	—		..	—
Box	,,	..	..	3 50	—	..	..	—
Bathampton	,,	..	..	3 58	—	..	..	—
Bath	,,	..	..	4 10	5 15	..	..	10 5
Temple Meads	arr.	..	..	4 45	5 35	..	..	10 25
Stapleton Road	arr.	..	..	..	..	..	..	..

K—Arrival time.

For details of full local service between Bristol and Bath, see page 5.

DIDCOT, SWINDON, BATH AND BRISTOL (Continued).

		A.M.	A.M.	A.M.	A.M.	A.M.	NOON.	A.M.	P.M.	P.M.
Stapleton Road	dep.	..	..	..	..	..	..	11 15	..	..
Temple Meads	,,	..	..	..	9 35	..	..	..	12 20	..
Bath	,,	..	9 0	..	9 58	..	..	11 47	12 42	..
Bathampton	,,	..	9 6	..	—	..	..	—	—	..
Box	,,	..	9 14	..	—	..	..	—	—	..
Corsham	,,	..	9 25	..	—	..	..	—	—	..
Chippenham	,,	..	9 33	..	10 20	10 30	..	12 10	1 8	1 45
Dauntsey	,,	..		..	10 30	10 40	..	—	—	1 55
Wootton Bassett	,,	..	..	..	10 40	10 52	..	—	—	2 5
Swindon	arr.	..	..	..	10 50	11 2	..	12 35	1 33	2 15
	dep.	8 58	..	9 30	11 0		12 0	12 45		
Shrivenham	,,	—	..	9 40	—	..	12 10	—	..	..
Uffington	,,	—	..	9 50	—	..	12 20	—	..	..
Challow	,,	—	..	10 0	—	..	12 30	—	..	..
Wantage Road	,,	—	..	10 10	—	..	12 40	—	..	..
Steventon	,,	—	..	10 20	—	..	12 50	—	..	..
Didcot	arr.	9 25	..	10 30	11 25	..	1 0	1 10	..	..
Paddington	arr.	10 35	..	12 45	1 10	..	..	3 0	..	..

		P.M.	P.M.	P.M.	P.M.	P.M.	P.M.	P.M.		
Stapleton Road	dep.	..	..	..	..	4 15	..	..	..	..
Temple Meads	,,	..	3 15	3 50	..	..	6 0	7 50	..	..
Bath	,,	..	3 40	4 20	..	4 40	6 40	8 15	..	..
Bathampton	,,	..	—	4 25	..	—	6 46	—	..	..
Box	,,	..	—	4 55	..	—	6 56	—	..	..
Corsham	,,	..	—	4 45	..	—	7 6	—	..	..
Chippenham	,,	..	4 5	5†15	..	5 5	7 20	8 45	..	..
Dauntsey	,,	..	—	5 25	..	—	7 30	..	..	..
Wootton Bassett	,,	..	—	5 35	..	—	7 40	—	..	..
Swindon	arr.	..	4 28	5 45	..	5 30	7 50	9 10	..	..
	dep.	3 0	4 38		4 50	5 40		9 20	..	..
Shrivenham	,,	3 10	—	..	5 0	—	..	—	..	..
Uffington	,,	3 20	—	..	5 10	—	..	—	..	..
Challow	,,	3 30	—	..	5 20	—	..	—	..	..
Wantage Road	,,	3 40	—	..	5 30	—	..	—	..	..
Steventon	,,	3 50	—	..	5 40	—	..	—	..	..
Didcot	arr.	4 0	5 15	..	5 50	6 5	..	9 45	..	..
Paddington	arr.	..	7 0	..	..	8 0	..	11 25	..	..

† Arrive Chippenham 4.53 p.m.

For details of full local service between Bristol and Bath see page 5.

SWINDON, BADMINTON AND BRISTOL.

		P.M.
Swindon	dep.	3 0
Wootton Bassett	,,	3 10
Brinkworth	,,	3 20
Little Somerford	,,	3 30
Hullavington	,,	3 40
Badminton	,,	3 55
Chipping Sodbury	,,	4 7
Coalpit Heath	,,	4 15
Winterbourne	,,	4 20
Filton Junction	,,	4 28
Ashley Hill	,,	4 34
Bristol—		
Stapleton Road	,,	4 40
Lawrence Hill	,,	4 45
Temple Meads	arr.	4 49

		P.M.
Bristol—		
Temple Meads	dep.	7 0
Lawrence Hill	,,	7 4
Stapleton Road	,,	7 7
Ashley Hill	,,	7 12
Filton Junction	,,	7 20
Winterbourne	,,	7 30
Coalpit Heath	,,	7 40
Chipping Sodbury	,,	7 48
Badminton	,,	8 0
Hullavington	,,	8 12
Little Somerford	,,	8 22
Brinkworth	,,	8 32
Wootton Bassett	,,	8 45
Swindon	arr.	8 55

BRISTOL, WESTON-SUPER-MARE, HIGHBRIDGE AND TAUNTON.

Station		A.M.	A.M.	A.M.	A.M.	A.M.	P.M.	P.M.	P.M.	
Temple Meads ..	dep.	9 0	9 35	10 45	..	11 0	12 10	1 0	1 45	..
Bedminster	„	9 5	9 40	—	..	11 5	12 15	1 5	—	..
Flax Bourton ..	„	9 15	9 49	—	..	11 14	12 24	1 14	—	..
Nailsea & Backwell	„	9 21	9 55	—	..	11 20	12 30	1 20	—	..
Yatton	„	9 30	10 5	—	..	11 28	12 40	1 30	—	..
Clevedon	arr.	9 38	10 38	—	..	11 46	12 58	1 43	—	..
Puxton and Worle	dep.	..	10 15	—	..	..	12 48	1 38	—	..
Weston-s.-Mare	arr.	..	10 23	11 10	..	..	12 55	1 45	2 12	..
	dep.	..		11 15	11 30	..			2 15	..
Bleadon & Uphill..	„	..	..	—	11 35	..	..	..	—	..
Brent Knoll	„	..	..	—	11 42	..	..	..		..
Highbridge	„	..	..	11 30	11 51	..	..	..	2 30	..
Bridgwater	arr.	..	..	11 45	12 5	..	..	..	2 40	..
Taunton	„	..	..	12 15	12 30	..	..	..	2 50	..
Exeter	„	..	..	1 0		..	..	..	3 40	..
Newton Abbot ..	„	..	..	1 30	..	..	..	..	**4K**20	..
Plymouth	„	..	..		**P**	..	..	..	5 40	..

Station		P.M.	P.M.	P.M.	P.M.	P.M.	P.M.	P.M.	P.M.	P.M.
Temple Meads ..	dep.	3 0	3 55	..	4 15	5 30	5 45	5 50	6 50	8 30
Bedminster	„	3 5	—	..	4 20	5 35	—	5 55	6 55	8 35
Flax Bourton	„	3 14	—	..	4 29	5 44	—	6 4	7 4	8 44
Nailsea & Backwell	„	3 20	—	..	4 35	5 50	—	6 10	7 10	8 50
Yatton	„	3 30	4 15	..	4 45	6 0	—	6 20	7 20	9 0
Clevedon	arr.	3 45	..	..	5 8	8 38	..	6 38	..	..
Puxton and Worle	dep.	3 38	—	..	4 53	6 8	—	..	7 28	9 8
Weston-s.-Mare	arr.	3 45	4 27	**P**	5 0	6 15	—	..	7 35	9 15
	dep.		4 35	4 50			..	—		
Bleadon & Uphill..	dep.	..	—	4 55	..	..	—	..	..	..
Brent Knoll	„	..	—	5 2	..	..	—	..	..	..
Highbridge	„	..	4 55	5 11	..	..	—	..	..	..
Bridgwater	arr.	..	5 5	5 25	..	..	—	..	..	..
Taunton	„	..	5 35	5 50	..	..	6 40	..	..	..
Exeter	„	..	6 20		..	..	7 20	..	..	..
Newton Abbot ..	„	..		..	..	..	7 50	..	..	..
Plymouth	„	..	**W**	..	..	..	8 40	..	..	..

K—This train will call at all Stations between Newton Abbot and Plymouth.

P—This train will call at all Stations between Highbridge and Taunton.

W—There will be a connection off this train from Exeter to Newton Abbot, calling at all Stations except Dawlish Warren.

TAUNTON, HIGHBRIDGE, WESTON-SUPER-MARE AND BRISTOL.

Station		A.M.	A.M.	A.M.	A.M.	A.M.	A.M.	A.M.	A.M.	P.M.
*Plymouth	dep.	..	..	..	..	..	..	..	..	..
Newton Abbot ..	„	..	..	..	..	**C**	..	..	..	..
Exeter	„	..	..	..	..	..	..	..	10 0	..
Taunton	„	..	..	..	..	9 30	..	..	10 50	..
Bridgwater	„	..	..	..	..	9 52	..	..	11 15	..
Highbridge	dep.	..	..	..	..	10 8	..	..	11 30	..
Brent Knoll	„	..	..	..	..	10 16	..	..	—	..
Bleadon and Uphill	„	..	..	..	..	10 24	..	..	—	..
Weston-super-Mare	arr.	..	..	..	..	10 30	..	..	11 50	..
	dep.	..	8 30	..	9 35		11 0	..	12 0	1 40
Puxton & Worle ..	dep.	..	8 37	..	9 42	..	11 7	..	—	1 47
Clevedon	dep.	8 5	—	..	9 43	..	11 5	11 50	..	1 15
Yatton	dep.	8 20	8 45	9 10	9 55	..	11 15	12 0	—	1 55
Nailsea & Backwell	„	8 28	8 53	9 18	10 3	..	11 23	12 8	..	2 3
Flax Bourton ..	„	8 34	8 59	9 24	10 9	..	11 29	12 14	—	2 9
Bedminster	„	8 44	9 9	9 34	10 19	..	11 39	12 24	—	2 19
Bristol (T.M.) ..	arr.	8 54	9 19	9 44	10 23	..	11 49	12 34	12 40	2 29

Station		A.M.	P.M.	P.M.	P.M.	P.M.	P.M.	P.M.	P.M.	
Plymouth	dep.	9**B**25	..	..	12**C**30	..	..	..	..	..
Newton Abbot ..	„	11 0	..	..	1 30	..	..	4 30	..	..
Exeter	„	11 50	..	..	2 0	..	..	5 10	..	..
Taunton	„	1 0	..	..	3 0	..	..	6 20	..	..
Bridgwater	„	1 20	..	..	3 25	..	..	6 45	..	..
Highbridge	dep.	1 48	..	..	3 38	..	..	7 0	..	..
Brent Knoll	„	—	..	..	3 46	..	..	—	..	..
Bleadon & Uphill..	„	—	..	..	3 54	..	..	—	..	..
Weston-s.-Mare	arr.	2 2	..	..	4 0	..	..	7 15	..	..
	dep.	2 10	2 50	..		4 30	5 45	7 20	8 10	..
Puxton & Worle ..	„	—	2 57	..	..	4 37	5 52	—	8 17	..
Clevedon	dep.	..	2 55	..	..	4 35	5 50	..	..	..
Yatton	dep.	—	3 5	3 45	..	4 45	6 0	..	8 25	..
Nailsea & Backwell	„	—	3 13	3 53	..	4 53	6 8	..		..
Flax Bourton ..	„	—	3 19	3 59	..	4 59	6 15	—	..	..
Bedminster	„	—	3 20	4 9	..	5 9	6 25	—	..	..
Bristol (T.M.) ..	arr.	2 40	3 39	4 19	..	5 19	6 35	7 45	..	..

B This train calls at all stations between Plymouth and Newton Abbot.

C This train will call at all stations between Taunton and Weston-super-Mare.

SALISBURY, BATH AND BRISTOL.

		A.M.	A.M.	A.M.	P.M.	P.M.	P.M.	P.M.
Salisbury..	dep.	8 30	..	11 30	4 15	5 30	6 20	..
Wilton	„	8 37	..	11 37	4 22	5 37	6 27	..
Wishford..	„	8 43	..	11 43	4 28	5 43	6 33	..
Wylye	„	8 52	..	11 52	4 37	5 52	6 42	..
Codford ..	„	9 0	..	12 0	4 45	6 0	6 50	..
Heytesbury	„	9 6	..	12 6	4 51	6 6	6 56	..
Warminster	„	9 16	..	12 16	5 1	6 16	7 6	..
Westbury	„	9 30	10 35	12 30	5 15	6 25	7 15	7 25
Trowbridge	„	9 45	10 48	12 43	5 28			7 38
Bradford-on-Avon	„	9 54	10 57	12 52	5 37	..	..	7 47
Freshford	„	10 0	11 3	12 58	5 43	..	..	—
Limpley Stoke	„	10 4	11 7	1 2	5 47	..	..	—
Bathampton ..	„	10 12	11 15	1 10	5 55	..	..	—
Bath..	„	10 20	11 22	1 18	6 3	..	..	8 10
Bristol (Temple Meads)	arr.	10 55	11 57	1 53	6 38	..	..	8 30

		A.M.	A.M.	P.M.	P.M.	P.M.	P.M.	
Bristol (Temple Meads)	dep.	..	11 20	1 30	3 30	5 0	9 0	..
Bath..	„	..	11 55	2 10	4 10	5 40	9 25	..
Bathampton	„	..	12 0	2 15	4 15	5 45	—	..
Limpley Stoke	„	..	12 8	2 23	4 23	5 53	—	..
Freshford	„	..	12 12	2 27	4 27	5 57	..	..
Bradford-on-Avon	„	..	12 18	2 33	4 33	6 3	9 40	..
Trowbridge	„	..	12 28	2 43	4 43	6 13	9 50	..
Westbury	„	9 0	12 40	2 55	4 55	6 25	9 58	..
Warminster	„	9 15	12 53	3 8	5 8	6 38		..
Heytesbury	„	9 23	1 1	3 16	5 16	6 46	..	..
Codford ..	„	9 30	1 8	3 23	5 23	6 53	..	..
Wylye	„	9 38	1 16	3 31	5 31	7 1	..	..
Wishford..	„	9 47	1 25	3 40	5 40	7 10	..	..
Wilton	„	9 53	1 31	3 46	5 46	7 16	..	..
Salisbury..	arr.	10 0	1 38	3 53	5 53	7 23	..	..

BRISTOL AND BATH.

		A.M.	A.M.	A.M.	A.M.	A.M.	P.M.	P.M.	P.M.	P.M.	P.M.
BRISTOL—											
Stapleton Road	dep.	..	..	..	11 15	..	..	..	..	..	..
Temple Meads	„	7 45	9 35	10 30	..	11 20	12 20	12 35	1 0	1 30	3 15
St. Anne's Park ..	„	7 50	—	10 35	—	11 25	—	12 40	1 5	1 35	—
Keynsham	„	8 0	—	10 45	—	11 35	—	12 50	1 15	1 45	—
Saltford	„	8 7	—	10 55	—	11 45	—	1 0	1 25	1 55	—
Bath	„	8 15	9 53	11 3	11 40	11 53	12 38	1 10	1 35	2 5	3 35

		P.M.	P.M.	P.M.	P.M.	P.M.	P.M.	P.M.	P.M.	P.M.	
BRISTOL—											
Stapleton Road	dep.	..	..	4 15	..	..	..	..	..	..	..
Temple Meads	„	3 30	3 50	..	4 20	5 0	6 0	6 30	7 50	9 0	..
St. Anne's Park ..	„	3 35	3 55	—	4 25	5 5	6 5	6 35	—	—	..
Keynsham	„	3 45	4 3	—	4 35	5 15	6 15	6 45	—	—	..
Saltford	„	3 55	4 10	—	4 45	5 25	6 25	6 55	—	—	..
Bath	arr.	4 5	4 17	4 35	4 55	5 35	6 35	7 5	8 15	9 20	..

BATH AND BRISTOL.

		A.M.	A.M.	A.M.	A.M.	A.M.	P.M.	P.M.	P.M.	P.M.	P.M.
Bath	dep.	8 30	10 20	10 40	11 22	11 45	12 0	12 20	12 58	1 18	1 45
Saltford	„	8 38	10 30	10 50	11 32	11 55	—	—	1 8	1 28	1 55
Keynsham	„	8 45	10 40	11 0	11 42	12 5	—	—	1 18	1 38	2 5
At. Anne's Park	„	8 55	10 50	11 10	11 52	12 15	—	—	1 28	1 48	2 15
BRISTOL—											
Temple Meads	arr.	9 0	10 55	11 15	11 57	12 20	..	12 40	1 33	1 55	2 20
Stapleton Road	„	..	..	..	..	..	12 20	..	..	..	..

		P.M.	P.M.	P.M.	P.M.	P.M.	P.M.	P.M.	P.M.		
Bath	dep.	2 30	4 10	5 15	5 30	6 3	7 30	8 10	10 5	..	..
Saltford	„	2 40	4 20	—	5 40	6 13	7 40	—	—	..	..
Keynsham	„	2 50	4 30	—	5 50	6 23	7 59	—	—	—	..
St. Anne's Park	„	3 0	4 40	—	6 0	6 33	8 0	—	—	..	..
BRISTOL—											
Temple Meads	arr.	3 5	4 45	5 35	6 5	6 38	8 5	8 30	10 25	..	..
Stapleton Road	„	..	..	..	..	..	..	..	..	..	..

CHIPPENHAM, WESTBURY AND WEYMOUTH.

		NOON.	P.M.	P.M.	P.M.	P.M.	P.M.	
Swindon	dep.	..	..	2 40	4 35	..	..	..
Chippenham ..	„	..	..	3 15	5 10	6 15	..	..
Melksham	„	..	..	3 29	5 25	6 30	..	..
Holt Junction	„	..	..	3 37	5 33	6 38	..	..
Trowbridge	„	..	..	3 48	5 45	6 48	..	..
Westbury	„	12 0	2 15	4 0	5 58	6 56	7 0	..
Frome	„	12 15	2 30	4 10	6 10		7 15	..
Witham	„	12 27	—		—	..	7 27	..
Bruton	„	12 37	2 50	..	6 30	..	7 37	..
Castle Cary ..	„	12 47	3 0	..	6 40	..	7 47	..
Marston Magna	„	12 57	—	..	—	..	7 57	..
Sparkford	„	1 6	—	..	—	..	8 6	..
Yeovil (Pen Mill)	„	1 20	3 25	..	7 5	..	8 20	..
Yetminster	„	1 35	—	..	—	..	8 30	..
Evershot	„	1 50	—	..	—	..	8 42	..
Maiden Newton	„	2 4	3 50	..	7 30	..	8 50	..
Grimstone	„	2 14	—	..	—	..	9 0	..
Dorchester	„	2 27	4 4	..	7 45	..	9 10	..
Upwey Junction	„	2 37	—	..	—	..	9 18	..
Weymouth	arr.	2 45	4 20	..	8 1	..	9 23	..

		A.M.	A.M.	A.M.	A.M.	P.M.	P.M.	P.M.
Weymouth	dep.	..	8 55	10 30	11 45	..	4 55	5 10
Upwey Junction	„	..	9 4	—	—	..	—	5 20
Dorchester	„	..	9 19	10 50	12 0	..	5 15	5 35
Grimstone	„	..	9 29	—	—	..	—	5 48
Maiden Newton	„	..	9 41	11 8	12 15	..	5 38	6 2
Evershot	„	..	9 52	—	—	..	—	6 15
Yetminster	„	..	10 4	—	—	..	—	6 30
Yeovil (Pen Mill)	„	..	10 19	11 35	12 42	..	6 5	6 45
Sparkford	„	..	10 29	—	—	..	—	6 58
Marston Magna	„	..	10 39	—	—	..	—	7 10
Castle Cary	„	..	10 49	11 55	12 59	..	6 25	7 20
Bruton	„	..	10 59	12 5	1 9	..	6 40	7 30
Witham	„	..	11 12	—	—	..	—	7 42
Frome	„	..	11 25	12 30	1 25	5 0	7 5	7 55
Westbury	„	9 20	11 40	12 50	1 40	5 15	7 25	8 5
Trowbridge	„	9 35		1 5		5 27	7 38	
Holt Junction	„	9 42	..	1 15	..	5 34		..
Melksham	„	9 52	..	1 25	..	5 45	..	..
Chippenham	arr.	10 5	..	1 37	..	5 57	..	..
Swindon	arr.	11 2	..	2 15	..	..	..	..

RAIL MOTOR CAR SERVICE, WEYMOUTH AND DORCHESTER.

		A.M.	A.M.	P.M.	P.M.	P.M.
Weymouth	dep.	8 0	10 0	1 0	3 30	5 45
Dorchester	arr.	8 25	10 25	1 25	3 55	6 10

		A.M.	A.M.	P.M.	P.M.	P.M.
Dorchester	dep.	8 35	11 0	1 45	4 15	6 15
Weymouth	arr.	9 0	11 25	2 10	4 40	6 40

SAVERNAKE AND WESTBURY.

		A.M.	P.M.	P.M.	
Savernake	dep.	10 47	4.30 p.m. ex Paddington.	7 15	..
Pewsey	„	10 57		7 25	..
Woodborough	„	11 4		7 32	..
Patney & Chirton	„	11 11		7 40	..
Devizes	„	11 22		—	..
Seend	„	11 31		—	..
Holt Junction	„	11 39		—	..
Trowbridge	„	11 45		—	..
Lavington	„	..		7 50	
Edington & Bratton	„	..		8 5	
Westbury	arr.	..	6 55	8 15	

		C	A	B	
		A.M.	P.M.	P.M.	P.M.
Westbury	dep.	11 40	1 40	..	4 0
Edington & Bratton	„	11 50	—	..	Reading arr. 5.20 p.m. Paddington arr. 6.15 p.m.
Lavington	„	12 3	—	..	
Trowbridge	„	—	..	3 20	
Holt Junction	„	—	..	3 30	
Seend	„	—	..	3 40	
Devizes	„	—	..	3 55	
Patney & Chirton	„	12 15	—	4 6	
Woodborough	„	12 25	—	4 12	
Pewsey	„	12 35	—	4 20	
Savernake	arr.	12 45	2 15	4 28	

A—Through train to Paddington, calling at stations between Savernake and Newbury, and at Reading, Maidenhead, West Drayton and Ealing (Broadway).

B—This train will run to Reading and call at all stations.

C—Through train to Paddington calling at all stations.

SWINDON, GLOUCESTER AND CHELTENHAM.

		A.M.	A.M.	NOON.	P.M.	P.M.	P.M.
Swindon	dep.	7 43	9 10	12 0	2 40	3 0	7 30
Purton	„	7 52	9 19	12 9	—	3 9	7 39
Minety	„	8 2	9 28	12 19	—	3 19	7 49
Kemble	„	8 16	9 40	12 33	3 2	3 33	8 3
Chalford	„	8 29	9 53	12 46	—	3 46	8 16
Brimscombe	„	8 34	9 59	12 51	—	3 51	8 21
Stroud	„	8 43	10 7	1 0	3 25	4 0	8 30
Stonehouse	„	8 50	10 15	1 7	—	4 7	8 37
Gloucester	arr.	9 5	10 30	1 22	3 45	4 22	8 52
Cheltenham (St. James)	„	—	11 2	2 15	—	5 41	—

		A.M.	A.M.	P.M.	P.M.	P.M.	
Cheltenham (St. James)	dep.	8 55	11 30	1 45	—	—	..
Gloucester	„	9 30	12 0	2 8	4 0	5 30	..
Stonehouse	„	9 45	12 15	2 22	4 15	5 45	..
Stroud	„	9 54	12 26	2 31	4 24	5 54	..
Brimscombe	„	10 0	12 33	2 38	4 31	6 1	..
Chalford	„	10 4	12 37	2 42	4 35	6 5	..
Kemble	„	10 21	12 56	3 0	4 54	6 24	..
Minety	„	10 30	1 5	3 9	5 3	6 33	..
Purton	„	10 37	1 13	3 18	5 11	6 41	..
Swindon	arr.	10 45	1 25	3 26	5 30	6 50	..

GLOUCESTER, CHEPSTOW, NEWPORT, AND CARDIFF.

		A.M.	P.M.	NOON.	P.M.	P.M.
Swindon	dep.	7 43	—	12 0	2 40	3 0
Gloucester	„	9 15	1 0	2 15	4 0	7 0
Oakle Street	„	9 24	—	2 24	—	7 9
Grange Court	„	9 28	—	2 28	4 12	7 15
Newnham	„	9 37	1 17	2 37	4 21	7 23
Awre Junction	„	9 45	—	2 45	—	7 36
Lydney	„	9 59	1 31	2 59	4 35	7 43
Woolaston	„	10 7	—	3 7	—	7 54
Chepstow	arr.	10 20	1 45	3 20	4 49	8 2
Severn Tunnel Junction	„	10 34	—	3 34	—	8 16
Newport	„	10 56	2 10	3 56	5 14	8 45
Cardiff (General)	„	11 17	2 32	4 17	5 36	9 10

		A.M.	P.M.	P.M.	P.M.	
Cardiff (General)	dep.	9 5	1 30	4 10	5 45	..
Newport	„	9 34	1 55	4 30	6 7	..
Severn Tunnel Junction	„	10 20	2 30	4 55	6 32	..
Chepstow	„	10 39	2 49	5 13	6 50	..
Woolaston	„	10 50	3 1	5 26	7 3	..
Lydney	„	10 58	3 10	5 35	7 12	..
Awre Junction	„	11 7	3 20	5 44	7 21	..
Newnham	„	11 15	3 28	5 52	7 29	..
Grange Court	„	11 23	3 36	5 59	7 36	..
Oakle Street	„	11 28	3 42	6 4	7 41	..
Gloucester	„	11 36	3 50	6 12	7 49	..
Swindon	arr.	1 25	5 20	..	—	—

GLOUCESTER AND CHELTENHAM.

		A.M.	A.M.	A.M.	P.M.	P.M.	P.M.
Cheltenham (St. James)	dep.	7 40	8 55	11 30	1 45	6 37	8 30
Cheltenham (Malvern Road)	„	7 42	8 57	11 32	1 47	6 39	8 32
Churchdown	„	7 49	9 4	11 39	1 54	6 47	8 39
Gloucester	„	7 55	9 10	11 45	2 0	6 53	8 45

		A.M.	A.M.	P.M.	P.M.	P.M.	P.M.
Gloucester	dep.	8 20	10 45	1 5	2 0	5 25	7 10
Churchdown	„	8 27	10 52	1 12	2 7	5 32	7 17
Cheltenham (Malvern Road)	arr.	8 33	11 0	1 20	2 13	5 39	7 24
Cheltenham (St. James)	„	8 35	11 2	1 22	2 15	5 41	7 26

BRISTOL, NEWPORT AND CARDIFF.

		A.M.	P.M.	P.M.	P.M.	
Bristol—						
Temple Meads	dep.	11 30	..	6 5	7 30	..
Lawrence Hill	„	11 34	A	6 9	7 34	..
Stapleton Road	„	11 38	12 20	6 15	7 38	..
Patchway	„	11 50	—	6 25	7 50	..
Pilning	„	11 57	—	6 32	7 57	..
Severn Tunnel Junction	„	12 12	12 50	6 47	8 12	..
Magor	„	—	—	—	8 20	..
Llanwern	„	—	—	—	8 30	..
Newport	arr.	12 33	1 10	7 8	8 40	..
Cardiff	„	12 53	1 30	7 28	9 0	..

		A.M.	A.M.	P.M.	P.M.	P.M.
Cardiff	dep.	8 40	10 15	2 40	3 15	4 35
Newport	„	9 0	10 35	3 5	3 35	4 55
Llanwern	„	—	—	—	—	5 3
Magor	„	—	—	—	—	5 11
Severn Tunnel Junction	„	9 17	10 50	3 22	3 50	5 22
Pilning	„	9 32	—	3 37	—	4 37
Patchway	„	9 42	—	3 47	—	5 47
Bristol—						
Stapleton Road	arr.	9 52	11 13	3 57	4 15	5 57
Lawrence Hill	„	9 57	11 17	4 2	4 17	6 4
Temple Meads	„	10 3	B	4 8	B	6 8

A—Through train ex Paddington.
B—Through trains to Paddington.

BRISTOL, CLIFTON DOWN AND AVONMOUTH DOCK.

		A.M.	A.M.	A.M.	P.M.	P.M.	P.M.	P.M.	P.M.	P.M.	P.M.
Temple Meads	dep.	9 15	10 15	11 15	12 15	1 15	2 15	3 15	4 15	5 15	6 15
Lawrence Hill	„	9 20	10 20	11 20	12 20	1 20	2 20	3 20	4 20	5 20	6 20
Stapleton Road	„	9 25	10 25	11 25	12 25	1 25	2 25	3 25	4 25	5 25	6 25
Montpelier	„	9 30	10 30	11 30	12 30	1 30	2 30	3 30	4 30	5 30	6 30
Redland	„	9 33	10 33	11 33	12 33	1 33	2 33	3 33	4 33	5 33	6 33
Clifton Down	„	9 37	10 37	11 37	12 37	1 37	2 37	3 37	4 37	5 37	6 37
Sea Mills	„	9 44	10 44	11 44	12 44	1 44	2 44	3 44	4 44	5 44	6 44
Shirehampton	„	9 50	10 50	11 50	12 50	1 50	2 50	3 50	4 50	5 50	6 50
Avonmouth Dock	arr.	9 55	10 55	11 55	12 55	1 55	2 55	3 55	4 55	5 55	6 55

		A.M.	A.M.	P.M.	P.M.	P.M.	P.M.	P.M.	P.M.	P.M.	P.M.
Avonmouth Dock	dep.	10 10	11 10	12 10	1 10	2 10	3 10	4 10	5 10	6 10	7 10
Shirehampton	„	10 16	11 16	12 16	1 16	2 16	3 16	4 16	5 16	6 16	7 16
Sea Mills	„	10 23	11 23	12 23	1 23	2 23	3 23	4 23	5 23	6 23	7 23
Clifton Down	„	10 30	11 30	12 30	1 30	2 30	3 30	4 30	5 30	6 30	7 30
Redland	„	10 33	11 33	12 33	1 33	2 33	3 33	4 33	5 33	6 33	7 33
Montpelier	„	10 36	11 36	12 36	1 36	2 36	3 36	4 36	5 36	6 36	7 36
Stapleton Road	„	10 41	11 41	12 41	1 41	2 41	3 41	4 41	5 41	6 41	7 41
Lawrence Hill	„	10 45	11 45	12 45	1 45	2 45	3 45	4 45	5 45	6 45	7 45
Temple Meads	arr.	10 50	11 50	12 50	1 50	2 50	3 50	4 50	5 50	6 50	7 50

BRISTOL, CLIFTON BRIDGE AND PORTISHEAD.

		A.M.	A.M.	P.M.	P.M.	P.M.
Temple Meads	dep.	8 45	..	..	..	..
Bedminster	„	8 50	..	..	..	..
Clifton Bridge	„	9 0	11 0	1 0	3 0	5 30
Pill	„	9 15	11 15	1 15	3 15	5 45
Portbury	„	9 25	11 25	1 25	3 25	5 55
Portishead	arr.	9 30	11 30	1 30	3 30	6 0

		A.M.	NOON.	P.M.	P.M.	P.M.
Portishead	dep.	10 0	12 0	2 0	4 0	6 30
Portbury	„	10 8	12 8	2 8	4 8	6 38
Pill	„	10 18	12 18	2 18	4 18	6 48
Clifton Bridge	„	10 30	12 30	2 30	4 30	7B 0
Bedminster	„	..	..	..	..	7 10
Temple Meads	arr.	..	..	..	..	7 15

B—Departure time.

BRISTOL, CHEDDAR, WELLS AND SHEPTON MALLET.

		A.M.	P.M.
Bristol (Temple Meads)	dep.	11 0	5 50
Yatton	„	11 32	6 22
Congresbury	„	11 38	6 28
Sandford and Banwell	„	11 46	6 36
Winscombe	„	11 52	6 42
Axbridge	„	12 0	6 50
Cheddar	„	12 8	6 58
Draycott	„	12 15	7 5
Lodge Hill	„	12 24	7 14
Wookey	„	12 34	7 24
Wells	arr.	12 37	7 27
Shepton Mallet	„	12 57	7 47

		A.M.	P.M.	P.M.
Shepton Mallet	dep.	7 43	1 15	8 0
Wells	„	8 0	2 30	8 12
Wookey	„	8 6	2 36	
Lodge Hill	„	8 15	2 45	..
Draycott	„	8 23	2 53	..
Cheddar	„	8 32	3 2	..
Axbridge	„	8 41	3 11	..
Winscombe	„	8 49	3 19	..
Sandford and Banwell	„	8 55	3 25	..
Congresbury	„	8 3	3 33	..
Yatton	arr.	9 7	3 37	..
Bristol (T. Meads)	arr.	9 45	4 15	..

BRISTOL, RADSTOCK AND FROME.

		A.M.	P.M.
Frome	dep.	8 25	2 30
Mells Road	„	8 38	2 43
Radstock	„	8 50	2 55
Midsomer Norton and W.	„	8 57	3 2
Hallatrow	„	9 7	3 12
Clutton	„	9 15	3 20
Pensford	„	9 23	3 28
Whitchurch Halt	„	9 30	3 35
Brislington	„	9 38	3 43
Temple Meads	arr.	9 45	3 50

		A.M.	P.M.
Temple Meads	dep.	11 0	5 10
Brislington	„	11 8	5 18
Whitchurch Halt	„	11 15	5 25
Pensford	„	11 22	5 32
Clutton	„	11 32	5 42
Hallatrow	„	11 38	5 48
Midsomer Norton and W.	„	11 48	5 58
Radstock	„	11 58	6 8
Mells Road	„	12 10	6 20
Frome	arr.	12 25	6 35

CALNE BRANCH.

		P.M.
Chippenham	dep.	1 0
Calne	arr.	1 15

		A.M.	P.M.	P.M.
Calne	dep.	11 45	2 0	5 0
Chippenham	arr.	12 0	2 15	5 15

CLEVEDON BRANCH.

		A.M.	A.M.	A.M.	A.M.	P.M.	P.M.	P.M.	P.M.	P.M.	P.M.
Yatton	dep.	7 50	9 30	10 30	11 38	12 30	1 35	2 30	3 35	5 0	5 30
Clevedon	arr.	7 58	9 38	10 38	11 46	12 38	1 43	2 38	3 43	5 8	6 38

		A.M.	A.M.	A.M.	A.M.	P.M.	P.M.	P.M.	P.M.	P.M.	P.M.
Clevedon	dep.	8 A5	9 43	11 5	11 50	1 15	1 50	2 55	4 25	5 50	6 45
Yatton	arr.	8 13	9 51	11 13	11 58	1 23	1 58	3 3	4 33	5 58	6 53

A—Through train to Bristol (Temple Meads).

MARLBOROUGH BRANCH.

		A.M.	A.M.	P.M.	P.M.	P.M.	P.M.
Marlborough	dep.	10 18	11 25	12 25	1 48	4 8	6 55
Savernake	arr.	10 30	11 37	12 37	2 0	4 20	7 7

		A.M.	A.M.	P.M.	P.M.	P.M.	P.M.
Savernake	dep.	10 55	11 50	12 50	2 25	4 35	7 20
Marlborough	arr.	11 7	12 2	1 2	2 37	4 47	7 32

YEOVIL AND TAUNTON.

		A.M.
Taunton	dep.	9 40
Durston	„	9 55
Athelney	„	10 1
Langport West	„	10 16
Martock	„	10 27
Montacute	„	10 33
Yeovil Town	„	10 48
Yeovil (Pen Mill)	„	10 50

		A.M.
Yeovil (Pen Mill)	dep.	11 45
Yeovil Town	„	11 50
Montacute	„	12 3
Martock	„	12 12
Langport West	„	12 27
Athelney	„	12 37
Durston	„	12 47
Taunton	arr.	1 2

BRIDPORT BRANCH.

		A.M.	A.M.	P.M.
Bridport	dep.	8 30	11 30	4 45
Powerstock	„	8 40	11 40	4 55
Toller	„	8 50	11 50	5 5
Maiden Newton	arr.	8 55	11 55	5 10

		A.M.	P.M.	P.M.
Maiden Newton	dep.	10 0	2 0	6 0
Toller	„	10 6	2 6	6 6
Powerstock	„	10 16	2 16	6 16
Bridport	arr.	10 23	2 23	6 23

MELCOMBE REGIS AND PORTLAND.

		A.M.	A.M.	P.M.	P.M.	P.M.
Melcombe Regis	dep.	10 30	11 40	2 0	3 4	4 19
Westham Halt	„	10 33	11 43	2 3	3 7	4 22
Rodwell	„	10 36	11 46	2 6	3 10	4 25
Wyke Regis Halt	„	10 41	11 51	2 11	3 15	4 30
Portland	arr.	10 46	11 56	2 16	3 20	4 35

		A.M.	P.M.	P.M.	P.M.	P.M.
Portland	dep.	11 10	12 5	2 35	3 30	5 0
Wyke Regis Halt	„	11 16	12 11	2 41	3 36	5 6
Rodwell	„	11 22	12 17	2 47	3 42	5 12
Westham Halt	„	11 24	12 19	2 49	3 44	5 14
Melcombe Regis	arr.	11 26	12 21	2 51	3 46	5 16

CHELTENHAM SPA, SWINDON, MARLBOROUGH, ANDOVER AND SOUTHAMPTON.

		A.M.
Cheltenham Spa (Lansdown)	dep.	10 28
Cheltenham (South) & Leckhampton	„	10 34
Andoversford Junction	„	10 46
Andoversford and Dowdeswell	„	10 48
Withington	„	10 54
Chedworth	„	11 3
Foss Cross	„	11 7
Cirencester (Watermoor)	„	11 19
South Cerney	„	11 26
Cricklade	„	11 34
Swindon Town	„	11 53
		P.M.
Chiseldon	„	12 3
Ogbourne	„	12 12
Marlborough L.L.	„	12 22
Savernake H.L.	„	12 33
Grafton and B.	„	12 40
Collingbourne	„	12 49
Ludgershall	„	12 59
Weyhill	„	1 8
Andover Junction	arr.	1 15
	dep.	1 30
Romsey	dep.	1 58
Southampton West	arr.	2 15
Southampton Terminus	arr.	2 25

		P.M.
Southampton Terminus	dep.	4 42
Southampton West	„	4 50
Rodbridge	„	4 58
Romsey	„	5 9
Andover Junction	arr.	5 37
	dep.	5 40
Weyhill	dep.	5 48
Ludgershall	„	5 57
Collingbourne	„	6 3
Grafton and B.	„	6 12
Savernake H.L.	„	6 17
Marlborough L.L.	„	6 28
Ogbourne	„	6 38
Chiseldon	„	6 45
Swindon Town	arr.	6 51
Cricklade	„	7 7
South Cerney	„	7 15
Cirencester (Watermoor)	„	7 24
Chedworth	„	7 39
Withington	„	7 47
Andoversford Junction	„	7 53
Cheltenham (South) & Leckhampton	„	8 1
Cheltenham	„	8 5

Paddington Station, May 14th, 1926.

FELIX J. C. POLE, General Manager.

J. W. Arrowsmith Ltd., Printers, Quay Street, Bristol.

This notice is shown as 'until further notice', thus ending the need to produce *daily* notices showing the complete divisional service. However, with the ending of the Strike, a complete reissue headed 'Temporary Passenger Train Services' was made, dated Monday 17th May until further notice. This, unfortunately, is again a Roneo version and not suitable for reproduction. Comparison between it and the 13th May notice reveals the following major differences (space only allows a summary to be given):

Didcot, Swindon, Bath and Bristol (complete list of through trains)

am
7.15 Padd.-Bristol (via Badminton)
9.15 Padd.-Bristol
10.45 Padd.-Cheltenham
pm
1.15 Padd.-Bristol
2.45 Padd.-Bristol (via Devizes)
4.30 Padd.-Bristol
5.15 Padd.-Bristol
5.55 Padd.-Swindon
6.30 Padd.-Bristol
9.25 Padd.-Cardiff (via Gloucester)
am
12.00 Padd.-Bristol
12.55 Padd.-Cardiff (via Gloucester)

am
4.05 Bristol-Padd.
7.45 Bristol - Padd.
7.20 Cheltenham-Padd.
9.35 Bristol-Padd.
11.10 Bristol-Padd. (via Devizes)
11.45 Bristol-Padd.
pm
12.20 Bristol-Padd.
1.45 Bristol-Padd.
3.15 Bristol-Padd.
5.15 Bristol-Padd. (first stop Swindon)
6.00 Bristol-Padd.
8.12 Swindon-Padd.
7.32 Bristol-Padd.
10.42 Cardiff-Padd. (via Gloucester)

Swindon, Badminton and Bristol
Three trains in each direction.

Bristol, Weston, Highbridge and Taunton
Considerably extended. For example the 'down' page which required 17 timetable columns in the 13th May service now requires 27.

Salisbury, Bath and Bristol
Similarly, the 13th May service required 7 columns in each direction; now needs 14 columns (to Salisbury) and 20 columns (from Salisbury).

Bristol and Bath
33 trains from Bristol and 30 from Bath.

Chippenham, Westbury and Weymouth
Seven arrivals at, and eight departures from Weymouth, plus additional 'short' workings between Swindon and Trowbridge and in the Frome area.

Weymouth-Dorchester Railmotor
Identical service.

Savernake and Westbury
The through expresses are restored to the route.

Swindon, Gloucester and Cheltenham
Nine down and eight up trains. (12 between Gloucester and Cheltenham.)

Gloucester, Chepstow, Newport and Cardiff
Seven down and eight up trains.

Stratford-Cheltenham
One Wolverhampton-Bristol express each way.

Bristol, Newport and Cardiff
Twelve 'down' timetable columns and 11 'up', some of which are short workings between Bristol and Pilning or Severn Tunnel Jn.

Bristol, Clifton Down and Avonmouth Dock
Hourly service 7.15 am-9.15 pm ex Bristol and 8.10 am-10.10 pm ex Avonmouth. In addition there are four trains each way routed via Filton Jn and Henbury.

Portishead Branch
Eight trains each way.

Bristol-Wells-Shepton Mallett
Service now resumed to Witham, with two trains running Bristol-Bristol via Yatton, Wells and Frome. Several 'short' workings but only four trains each way Bristol-Wells (via Yatton).

Bristol, Radstock and Frome
Four trains to Frome, five to Bristol.

Calne Branch
Five trains each way.

Clevedon Branch
Fifteen trains each way.

Marlborough Branch
Eight (GW) trains each way, plus two each way on the M&SWJ.

Yeovil Branch
Four trains to Yeovil and three to Taunton, plus one 'short' SO working.

Bridport Branch
Four trains each way and running to West Bay resumed (three each way). However, the branch closed *earlier* than during the Strike, the last arrival at Bridport from Maiden Newton being at 5.11 pm.

Portland Branch
Nineteen trains each way, plus two SO (practically a full service?)

Cheltenham Spa-Southampton (M&SWJ)
Only one train each way throughout but several 'short' workings.

Re-opened services, not included in the 13th May timetable, are as follows:

Faringdon Branch
Four trains each way leaving Uffington between 8.36 am and 4.13 pm.

Highworth Branch
Three down and six up basic daily workings, plus some additional down trains on Saturdays only.

Malmesbury Branch
Five trains each way between 7.13 am (from Malmesbury) and 6.46 pm (last arrival at Malmesbury).

Blagdon Branch
8.15 am and 6.45 pm ex Yatton; 8.55 am and 7.25 pm ex Blagdon.

Trowbridge-Patney & Chirton (via Devizes)
Seven down and eight up trains.

Castle Cary-Taunton Stopping Service
Three trains each way.

Abbotsbury Branch
Three trains each way (last ex Abbotsbury 3.24 pm).

Tidworth Branch
Four trains each way.

Swindon Town Shuttle
Five trains to the Town and six back.

If nothing else, this lengthy list makes one realise just how many branch lines there used to be in the Bristol division!

The following weekend was the Whitsun Holiday weekend and the preserved notices show a modest number of additional express and branch trains run, so some holiday traffic must have been available. The sum total of the additional expresses shown is as follows. On Saturday 22nd May the 10.35 am Wolverhampton to Penzance was divided, the first part (to Penzance) running non-stop from Cheltenham to Taunton. The second part ran from Wolverhampton to Weston-super-Mare. Similarly the 10.30 am Penzance to Wolverhampton ran in two parts, the first part starting from Weston-super-Mare at 3.50 pm. On Tuesday 25th May the 8.15 am Plymouth to Paddington (via Bristol) was divided, the first part running as booked, the second part starting at Paignton and running to Bristol where it then formed the 12.55 pm Bristol to Bradford.

Chapter Seven

The Departments Report After the Strike

Some four weeks after the conclusion of the Strike, the GM asked the head of each department to write a brief history of the event as it affected that department. Some of the highlights of these reports* form the basis of this chapter.

Superintendent of the Line

Mr Nicholls considered that his daily reports to the GM, plus a memo dated 19th May, gave all the details and did not provide anything else. The 19th May report was mainly a bringing together of the more important facts described in the daily reports (see Appendix Two), but there are a few statements worth repeating here.

The company was called upon to provide seven special trains for the Ocean Liner passenger traffic and mails from Plymouth to Paddington 'and all requirements were satisfactorily catered for.'

The employment of volunteer signalmen in many boxes throughout the system 'contributed in no small measure to the successful development of the working during the Strike.' Ninety-two volunteer signalmen, trained at Paddington, were sent out at the beginning of the Strike and more followed later. Seventy-four guards and 138 shunters were also trained at Paddington.

At a meeting at the Railway Clearing House on 18th May the Superintendents agreed that they would not restore any excursions for the forthcoming Whitsun holiday, but that weekend tickets would be extended by one day until the Tuesday, and that 'a limited number of day and half-day excursions should be arranged for Whit Sunday and Monday only' (which seems to conflict with the first statement).

Chief Goods Manager

The outbreak of the Strike found the goods department with three to four days traffic on hand (approximately 50,000 loaded wagons!) and 95 per cent of the Conciliation staff on strike. Many of these wagons were in transit and were left, for the most part, on lines inaccessible to road transport (but there were no cases on the GWR of trains being dumped on running lines).

In each area, with the help of despatch riders and private cars loaned by traders and 'the company's patrons generally' the exact location and contents of each wagon was determined. Many traders assisted the company in distribution of urgent perishable traffic, 'with an enthusiasm largely spontaneous and certainly sincere', even when involving journeys of up to 50 miles to collect the traffic. In some cases formidable difficulties had to be overcome because of the inaccessibility of wagons containing foodstuffs (and of

*Records filed under RAIL786 at Kew.

course lack of shunting power to extract the most important loads). As an example of co-operation between loyal staff, volunteers and traders in one (unnamed) district, details were quoted of a daily average of 666 loads delivered totalling approximately 800 tons for each day of the Strike, of which over 90 per cent was carted by traders.

As things improved and shunting power became available, operations were extended. Some of the company's lorries were utilised, employing volunteers, and deliveries effected in areas of up to 15 miles radius of the depots. Some assistance was received from traders employing their own locomotives, and it was noted that the Oxfordshire Ironstone Company lent five sets of enginemen 'who were of great assistance'. At certain places petrol-engined shunting engines had given good results and 'if more of this type of power had been available, it could have been usefully employed.'

In a paragraph dealing with traffic from Ireland and the Channel Islands, it was noted that rail facilities at Fishguard had been unavailable, owing to closure of the line between Carmarthen and Swansea, and that the City of Cork Steam Packet Co's ship, together with the GWR Rosslare boat, had been unloaded at Fishguard by voluntary dockers and the traffic in part brought to Swansea by road, 'the remainder being handed over to the LMS at Carmarthen for forwarding.' The part of the previous sentence in quotes rates a pencil underline and two exclamation marks in the margin of the GWR bound volume (now at Kew) - obviously the GM was not best pleased by this! Cattle landed at Fishguard was put out to pasture. Subsequently the ships ran to Cardiff and the Rosslare steamer *St Patrick* which the company intended to run to Cardiff with only 50 tons of traffic, actually sailed with 200 tons, the balance obtained between the decision and the date of sailing.

At the beginning of the Strike the following employees of the department were out on strike:

	Employees	*No. on Strike*	*Percentage*
Clerical	3,777	906	23.98
Supervisory	677	357	52.73
Conciliation	8,491	8,134	95.79
Shopmen	299	297	99.33
Other Grades	473	238	50.32
	13,717	9,932	72.40

The report notes that the majority of strikers remained out throughout the whole period. The Goods department had not been much affected by the work sharing scheme subsequently developed, 'as the volume of general merchandise the company was called upon to handle was heavy, and, at some points, created congestion.' However, although there was, as yet, no appreciable decline in the quantities of goods passing, it was felt that a reduction was inevitable if the Coal Strike was not quickly settled, which would lead to the suspension of the guaranteed week in this department.

Road Transport Department

This report is divided into three sections, Horses, Omnibuses and Cartage Services.

Horses

In the smaller stables the men responsible for feeding largely remained at work, but in London and some other large centres the stables were almost entirely deserted. At *Paddington* the men requested a letter from the chief officers asking them to come in and look after the horses, but when this was declined all the staff, except two, walked out. Their places were taken by clerical staff, volunteers and employees of Messrs Tattersalls; some ladies were employed. At *Poplar* all the staff struck until the TUC called off the General Strike on 12th May; they were replaced by four volunteers who were bedded down and fed from Paddington.

There was a most peculiar situation at *South Lambeth* where all the staff remained at work until midday on Friday 14th May, when they went out on strike! (Were they 'got at'?) The four volunteers who had been holding the fort at Poplar were now sent to South Lambeth, presumably the resident work force returned on 17th May?

At *Manchester* all except the foreman were on strike; the latter, a man new to the post and the city, did a good job in obtaining voluntary help.

At Smithfield, Birmingham, Bristol, Cardiff (Goods & Passenger), Newport, Oxford, Plymouth the staff remained at work and looked after their horses. At small country stations practically all the carmen came in, and in many cases performed deliveries and collections.

The report ends, 'The feeding of the stud was cut down to half the usual ration and practically no sickness occurred through the horses standing in. This reduction saved a considerable sum of money.'

Omnibus Services

By 8th May at *Abergavenny* the service had grown to nine trips between Abergavenny and Brecon, in spite of a certain amount of intimidation experienced by the drivers. At *Bovey Tracey*, however, the service was suspended from 5th-11th May, although the Moretonhampstead bus was extended here from 7th May. A special service was run from *Falmouth* to Truro between 5th-15th May; *Haverfordwest* maintained all its normal routes, plus a couple of goods services on 4th-5th May. *Kingsbridge*, however, did not manage to resume full services until 7th May.

At *Llandyssul* staff remained loyal, fetching foodstuffs from Carmarthen (despite a hostile crowd there), as well as maintaining the passenger service. One driver, a former locomotive fireman, was released to take up his old duties on 10th May.

At *Neath* only the supervisor remained at work, and the hostility of the 'crowd' prevented any buses being run, even though the trains were also at a complete standstill. Eventually, on 12th May, two buses were moved to *Gloucester* where they worked a service to Cheltenham.

At *Paignton* only the supervisor was on duty, but by 8th May the normal schedules were being worked, presumably by volunteers. In addition special buses were run vice trains between Paignton and Kingswear (a route not normally served by buses) from 6th-17th May, and from Totnes to Buckfastleigh (on 6th and 7th May).

At *Penzance* one of the volunteer drivers was intimidated leading afterwards to the sacking of the staff involved (although later reinstated). One driver was released on 11th May for locomotive firing duties. At *St Austell* half the staff was on strike but volunteers enabled a full service to be run, plus a special service to Newquay and Truro and conveyance of perishables despite 'a good deal of obstruction.' At *Saltash* all the staff remained loyal.

At *Slough* it was possible to maintain a normal Windsor-Ascot service plus a special service to Windsor until the branch line resumed. At *Twyford* the service was discontinued after two days because the driver was loaned to the locomotive department training volunteers for engine driving, and the bus sent to Paddington.

Wantage was running a normal service from 10th May using volunteers, and *Weymouth* from 11th May, both places having run skeleton or partial services before that. At *Wrexham*, however, no service at all was possible.

At *Paddington* omnibuses were used for the special staff services to Ealing, Southall, Uxbridge and Windsor and it was considered that this should be 'registered as part of the emergency organisation' planning in future. Finally it was noted that at the following depots all staff remained loyal enabling normal services to run: Aberystwyth, Dolgelley, Haverfordwest, Llandyssul, Marlborough, Chagford, Pwllheli and Saltash.

Cartage Services

Practically the whole of the mechanical shop staff went on strike with the conspicuous exception of Birmingham, where nearly the whole of the men remained loyal. This enabled a heavy tonnage to be moved in the Birmingham district.

The only other place specifically mentioned is Paddington where only the mechanical foremen remained at work, but with the assistance of the mechanical inspectors, clerks and volunteers all the perishable traffic arriving at Paddington was delivered. Four of the volunteers, including a Mrs Talbot, had their 'vehicles stormed by the mob.'

In view of the lack of train services west of Swansea, road motors were of great use delivering foodstuffs in that area.

Chief Mechanical Engineer

At noon on Tuesday 4th May, the first full day of the Strike, only 70 train crews were available throughout the whole of the GWR. Swindon Works closed during the afternoon of that day because of the very limited number of employees who had reported for work. Few of the department's staff returned to work during the Strike, but the bulk of the supervisory staff remained at work.

The CME recorded that 'a large number of volunteers were pressing for regular employment with the company' and this would be considered when the Miners' strike was resolved.

Chief Engineer

Although, on average, nearly 89 per cent of the clerical and technical staff remained loyal, and 88 per cent of the supervisory staff, in the South Wales divisions the position was reversed and between 42 per cent (Neath) and 88 per cent (Newport Docks) of the clerical, etc. staff and between 38 per cent (Neath) and 57 per cent (Newport Docks) of the supervisors were on strike. The Newport division, however, was an exception and here only 11.5 per cent (clerical) and 12.5 per cent (supervisors) were on strike. The track grades were almost all out (93.7 per cent), but there were exceptions, particularly in the Gloucester and Shrewsbury divisions. At Cheltenham no less than 90 out of 117 permanent way men remained loyal, it was thought because of the personal influence of the local inspector.

The various incidents of vandalism, already described in Chapter Two are mentioned, but an additional snippet of information is that at Taff Bargoed an engineer's trolley was used to convey coal from an outcrop 'which had been worked surreptitiously on adjoining land' at Merthyr!

Signal Engineer

There was not much to report: practically the whole of the outdoor staff left work and, with very few exceptions, no linemen were available to maintain signalling apparatus. However, signalling inspectors, and 'squads of men from the office staff at Reading and Cardiff' carried out necessary repairs, keeping equipment working. At Reading Works 152 men remained loyal out of 344.

Staff on Strike	
Conciliation	1,768
Shop staff	267
Clerical	19
Supervisory	15
	2,069
Remained Loyal	422
	2,491

Stores Department

Despite 27 per cent of the clerks, 28 per cent of the supervisors and 69 per cent of the wages staff being on strike, the Stores Department continued to function throughout the Strike, with one exception. This latter was Didcot Provender Stores where no less than 45 out of 47 staff, including all 4 supervisors, were on strike. This may be because Didcot was a 'railway town' and the stores staff took their lead from the other grades. No wagons could be moved, nor work done, during the first week but a team of volunteers was arranged to man the machines used for chaff cutting and mixing, loading and unloading from the Monday of the second week.

Marine Department

The crews of the cross-Channel vessels remained at work but the staff of the Plymouth tenders, the Fishguard tug *Pen Cw* and the Dartmouth ferry *The Mew* all struck; the Plymouth crews were replaced by volunteers but the other two vessels mentioned were laid up for the duration.

Most of the Fishguard Harbour staff struck, including the coaling gang, although as all the vessels had been filled with coal before the Strike started this 'did not actually interfere with the running.' The Weymouth-Channel Islands service 'was fully maintained in consequence of our vessels being oil burners.'

One hundred and fourteen staff out of a total complement of 526 were on strike, but no clerical staff were involved. Capt. Sharpe, the Marine Superintendent, considered that the crews of the Fishguard tug, the Plymouth tenders and *The Mew* should be members of the National Seamen's and Firemen's Union (which was 'moderate' and not on strike), 'but under existing laws, that is not possible.'

Police Department

Some 12 hours before the Strike started, enrolment of special constables started and by the second day of the Strike almost the full complement had been enrolled, including over 500 men in the London area (of the GWR). Transport arrangements were laid on to relieve specials on duty at Park Royal, Old Oak Common, Wood Lane, Hammersmith and South Lambeth at 8 am, 4 pm and 12 midnight daily.

'The recruits represented many and varied walks in life, from the Peer of the Realm to the labourer, the general to the private, the famous King's Counsel to the humble Attorney, and a very valuable contingent drawn from the Company's clerical staff. But whatever their rank or station in public or private life, as Special Constables they were one and all imbued with the true British spirit of rendering any kind of service to their Company in its hour of need.' [The recipient of this report - thought to be the GM - who has previously made two handwritten amendments to correct grammatical errors has written the word 'country' above 'Company' in the last sentence quoted.]

The report includes a table showing the number of 'authorised' and 'enrolled' special constables, the 'enrolled' column of which totalled 2,202 specials, the largest contingents being: Paddington-Southall (598), Cardiff (257), Birmingham (162), Newport (75) and Bristol (68). Surprisingly Slough East-Windsor justified 48 men (59 men actually enrolled) while Reading only had 40 and Gloucester only enrolled 15 men (50 authorised).

Police escorts had been provided to accompany lorries from the various London depots and with the exception of some destinations in the East end, particularly Poplar, these escorts had worked successfully. Between 7th-14th May nearly 400 vans were escorted from Paddington passenger station. A special constable named Rees had been in charge of these escort arrangements and Mr Matthews, the chief of police, was obviously impressed as he quoted extensively from the former's report.

The report gives details of those prosecutions which had already taken place and includes the fascinating information that a 'signal engineer' (non-striking) had been fined 20s. for assaulting a junior striker, while a fireman from Aberdare had been sentenced to two months hard labour for possessing Communist literature!

Mr Matthews, who was obviously one of the 'old school', concludes with a homily on the nature of the Strike. He considered that although some of those involved were 'revolutionaries', 'two thirds of the (striking) staff . . . yielded to the fear of disobeying the dictates of Union officials.' He ended, 'If we persist in vigorously prosecuting our enquiries, and in those cases where the facts justify, take Police Court proceedings, it will teach wrong-doers a lesson which will make them more cautious . . . in future.'

Although a poor photograph (copied from the *Western Morning News*) this picture is included for its interest; it shows a volunteer 'unloading' parcels at Plymouth - by the look of it, the heaviest being placed on top of the lightest!

GREAT WESTERN RAILWAY.

TERMS OF SETTLEMENT AS BETWEEN THE RAILWAY COMPANIES ON THE ONE HAND AND THE NATIONAL UNION OF RAILWAYMEN, ASSOCIATED SOCIETY OF LOCOMOTIVE ENGINEERS & FIREMEN, AND THE RAILWAY CLERKS' ASSOCIATION ON THE OTHER.

1 Those employees of the Railway Companies who have gone out on strike to be taken back to work as soon as traffic offers and work can be found for them. The principle to be followed in reinstating to be seniority in each grade at each station, depot or office.

2. The Trade Unions admit that in calling a strike they committed a wrongful act against the Companies and agree that the Companies do not by reinstatement surrender their legal rights to claim damages arising out of the strike from strikers and others responsible.

3. The Unions undertake:—
   (a) not again to instruct their members to strike without previous negotiations with the Companies.
   (b) to give no support of any kind to their members who take any unauthorised action.
   (c) not to encourage Supervisory employees in the Special Class to take part in any strike.

4. The Companies intimated that arising out of the strike it may be necessary to remove certain persons to other positions, but no such person's salary or wages will be reduced. Each Company will notify the Unions within one week the names of men whom they propose to transfer and will afford each man an opportunity of having an advocate to present his case to the General Manager.

5. The settlement shall not extend to persons who have been guilty of violence or intimidation.

On behalf of the General Managers' Conference:—	*On behalf of the Railway Trade Unions*:—	
FELIX J. C. POLE.	J. H. THOMAS,	National Union of Railwaymen.
H. G. BURGESS.	C. T. CRAMP,	
H. A. WALKER.	J. BROMLEY,	Associated Society of Locomotive Engineers and Firemen.
R. L. WEDGWOOD.		
R. H. SELBIE.	A. G. WALKDEN,	Railway Clerks' Association.

Dated this Fourteenth Day of May, Nineteen Hundred and Twenty-six.

The terms of the settlement of the General Strike, signed by the five General Managers (including that of the Metropolitan Railway) and the three Trade Unions, 14th May, 1926.

Chapter Eight

The Aftermath - Victimisation?

The GWR had issued a statement as early as 7th May on victimisation, which was later made into a poster - *see illustration*. This said, quite clearly, that the company considered itself, and the country generally, the victim in this case, not the strikers.

From the early days of the Strike the company had decided that strikers who wished to return to work should be allowed to do so provided they could be usefully employed, but that supervisors and station masters should not be allowed to resume unless individually authorised by HQ at Paddington.

By 9th May numbers returning had increased, and after taking the advice of the Solicitor, the General Manager issued the infamous circular No. 3002. The Solicitor had advised that if the company took back a striker without some definite condition, this was tantamount to condoning the striker's breach of contract (by striking without notice). Only the GWR issued this document, although the LNER put out something similar.

Circular 3002 read as follows:

GENERAL MANAGER'S OFFICE,
PADDINGTON STATION, W.2.
May 9th, 1926
NOON

Circular No. 3002

REINSTATEMENT OF STRIKERS

From many stations throughout the line highly satisfactory reports have been received that men are returning to work. The instructions already issued in regard to the reinstatement of strikers remain in force, namely:

Until further notice men on strike who offer to return to work may be re-employed, provided that their services can be utilised in any capacity, but no man who is known to have taken a leading part in organising or carrying on the strike, nor any supervisor, is to be allowed to resume duty without explicit instructions from this office.

A period will be reached when sufficient staff will have returned to work to enable a satisfactory service to be maintained, but the injury to trade is expected to be so serious that for some considerable time work will not be available for the normal staff. When 50 per cent of the staff at any station have resumed duty any other men who are allowed to return must be handed a notice in the following terms:

"Mr...
Formerly employed as..
You are hereby re-engaged on the understanding that you are not relieved of the consequences of having broken your contract of service with the Company."

....
Officer in charge of Station or Depot

A list must be kept of the men to whom this notice is handed.

Men up to the limit of capacity must be re-engaged strictly in the order in which they present themselves, and on no account must men be put on in excess of what is necessary for the conduct of the business as may be arranged from day to day.

FELIX J.C. POLE,
General Manager.

GREAT WESTERN RAILWAY.

VICTIMISATION.

The word Victimisation has often been used in connection with Strikes. In the experience of the Great Western Railway, it has usually been imported at the end of a Strike, the Trade Unions invariably asking that there should be no victimisation. The present strike not only differs from previous strikes in that it is not associated with any dispute or Labour question affecting the Company, but because of the fact that victimisation started with the strike, the victim in this case being the Great Western Railway Company. It is indeed true to say that the Country as a whole is being victimised by a strike which is the blackest spot in the history of Labour in this country. That thousands of men with no grievance against their employers should have been "instructed" to leave work, and that so many of them should have done so passes all comprehension. It can only be explained on the ground that there was a deep conspiracy against the State. Thank God such a conspiracy cannot succeed and can only result in the discrediting of its promoters and the disillusionment of those who have been used as pawns in the game

F. H. Pole

General Manager.

PADDINGTON STATION,
May, 1926.

A poster issued by the GWR on the subject of Victimisation.

The reason for allowing 50 per cent of the staff back without the issue of the form was said to be because it was considered that, even with the loss of traffic, at least 50 per cent of the staff at a station etc. would be necessary. After that, 'the remainder should not be exonerated from liability for breach of contract . . .' This aspect does not appear to have been properly thought through and later, on 12th May, it was decided that *all* striking staff accepted for work should be issued with the form.

Sir Felix Pole (who was Chairman of the General Managers' Conference that year) was chairing a series of special meetings of the 'Big Four' GMs, plus the GM of the Metropolitan Railway. This met from 30th April to 13th May (it was held daily from 10th-13th May). On Monday 10th May, with the purpose of indicating to the Government the railway companies' expectation that they should be consulted before the Strike was settled, the General Managers drew up the following Minute:

No. 21 - TERMS OF SETTLEMENT OF STRIKE

The policy to be adopted at the termination of the general strike was fully discussed, and the following general principles were agreed:

(1) The Railway Companies ought not to be put under any general obligation to re-employ persons on strike except as and when they are actually required for the conduct of the business of the Companies.
(2) The re-employment of any person is to be on the understanding that the Railway Companies do not surrender their legal rights to claim damages arising out of the strike from strikers and others responsible.
(3) The Railway Companies to be at liberty to refuse to re-employ any person who has been guilty of acts of violence or intimidation, or who has wilfully damaged the property of his employers immediately prior to going on strike or whilst on strike.
(4) The Railway Companies ought not to be committed to the re-employment of Station Masters, Goods Agents and others who, having held positions of special responsibility, have joined in the strike.

This information was passed to the Government by the Railway Companies Association, and, in addition, Lord Churchill, the GWR's Chairman, handed a copy to the Prime Minister, Stanley Baldwin.

At the same meeting the General Managers debated three proposals which had been placed before them by the Railways Staff Conference (RSC) (the top body discussing personnel matters in the railway industry):

1. Strikers should only be re-employed at standard, or base, rates and treated as new entrants. [This would mean that the companies would no longer be bound to apply old-established Terms and Conditions.]
2. All men who remained loyal to continue to receive existing rates of pay; and conditions of service.
3. The present scheme [negotiating machinery introduced in 1920] should be withdrawn and be replaced by a 'scheme on the lines of the 1907 Conciliation Scheme . . . established in its place.'

Unfortunately the Minutes do not record the discussion on these very controversial proposals, but items 1 and 2 were referred back to the RSC for further consideration, while item 3 was deferred for consideration at a later date.

On Wednesday 12th May the General Strike was called off by the TUC, with effect from midnight. However the effect of circular 3002 on the GWR meant that the SOL office took a succession of telephone calls from divisional superintendents on Wednesday evening and overnight. These intimated that the men would not return to work under the terms of circular 3002 (*see also Chapter Two*). A similar hard line attitude by the other companies ensured that, although the General Strike finished, what became known as the 'Railway Strike' took its place without a break.

The Government was becoming concerned at the tough line being adopted by the railways, and at 9.30 pm on 12th May the Minister of Labour called a meeting of the railway companies in the House of Commons. Here he emphasised the need to follow the advice given by the Prime Minister in the House earlier in the day that 'we should resume our work in the spirit of co-operation, putting behind us all malice and vindictiveness.'

Sir Guy Granet, Chairman of the LMSR, put the railways' point of view and emphasised the need to restore discipline following the 'unfortunate experience of recent years of strikes and strike settlements.' Sir Felix Pole took the opportunity of reviewing the four points made by the GMs in their Minute of 10th May. The government representative expressed 'full sympathy with these points, as also the need for the restoration of discipline.'

As recorded in Chapter Two, it was necessary to telephone Sir Felix Pole at 1.30 am on Thursday 13th May, and the GM decided that men would be allowed to return to work (if required) even though they would not sign for circular 3002. However, he said, the men must understand the terms of the form before being allowed to resume. This did not have the desired effect, however, and men continued refusing to book on unless all their colleagues could be taken back.

The General Managers met on Thursday 13th May and in the light of communications received from the three main rail unions, for example expressing surprise that 'great difficulties are being placed in the return to duty' (NUR), or, 'My Executive have instructed men to continue on strike until allowed to resume work unconditionally' (ASLEF), issued the notice setting out their terms (*see illustration on page 42*). Note the reference to rumours having been circulated that men would only be taken back at wage reductions as being 'absolutely incorrect' - although we know from the Minutes of 10th May that this had certainly been considered!

That afternoon a letter was received by Sir Felix Pole from the three railway unions asking for an early meeting. This was arranged with the General Managers' Committee and started at 6 pm. After lengthy discussions, the following initial draft terms of settlement was handed to the union representatives:

1. Those employees of the Railway Companies who have gone out on strike to be taken back to work as soon as traffic offers and work can be found for them.
2. In order to facilitate the early return of all men possible:

(a) The Guaranteed Week for those classes of employees covered by the agreements with the Railway Companies to which the National Union of Railwaymen are parties, to be suspended forthwith, but to be restored as soon as traffic becomes normal.
(b) Work available to be distributed as far as reasonably possible so as to equalise the number of days' work for each man.
(c) The Companies as far as possible to arrange holidays during the suspension of the Guaranteed Week.

3. Each person as taken back to be reinstated in the position he held prior to the strike.
4. Each weekly paid person who has gone on strike to forfeit a week's wages at normal rates. Each monthly paid person to forfeit one-fourth of a month's salary.
5. This arrangement is not to apply to:
(a) Persons who have been guilty of violence or intimidation.
(b) Persons in supervisory grades, including Station Masters, Goods Agents, and Clerks in Special Class and Class 1; but each such case is to be separately considered and decided by the Companies.

The Trade Unions agree that each man who left his work without notice has broken his contract of service, and that the Companies do not by reinstatement surrender any rights that they may possess.

Discussion continued until 10 pm, resuming at 10.30 am the next day. It was agreed that the reference to the Guaranteed Week should be removed, and that this would be dealt with separately in the event of the Coal Strike continuing. Eventually, the companies agreed to drop the forfeiture of a week's pay and the exclusion of the supervisory grades from the terms of the settlement. The final terms of the settlement, *illustrated on page 96*, were signed at 4.30 pm on 14th May. For their part the Unions had admitted 'a wrongful act' and acknowledged the right of the companies to claim damages.

Hastening back to Paddington, Sir Felix Pole called a meeting of the Chief Officers' Conference. The terms were explained and it was decided that circular 3002 could be withdrawn. The administration of clause 4 would be left to 'Heads of Departments.' 'The Officers heartily congratulated the General Manager on having arrived at such a satisfactory settlement. It was recognised that this was largely due to his own personal efforts and they desired to record their appreciation of the valuable service he had rendered not only to his own Company but to all Companies.' Thus ended the two-day 'Railway Strike.'

Before looking at the question of victimisation on the GWR it is as well to consider the prevailing atmosphere as the country slowly staggered back to work. In his book *The General Strike* G.A. Phillips writes:

. . . the Government's conduct towards its own employees was at least as harsh as that meted out by the majority of private employers. The Treasury recommended, and the Cabinet agreed, that government industrial workers should be reinstated only when work becomes available; that they should, where eligible, forfeit one year's service in respect of pension or gratuity rights; that those guilty of violence or intimidation . . . should be dismissed and that the men's 'accredited representatives' should be compelled to acknowledge that the stoppage was 'a wrongful act' [sounds familiar?].

So far as the local authorities were concerned:

8035

APPENDIX "A." (Minute 10527.)

This form to be used in connection with the appointment of all Supervisory Staff.

A.

105

Great Western Railway.

On appointment to the Supervisory Staff, I, the undersigned, undertake :—

(1) To do everything within my power to promote the best interests of the Company and efficiently to perform the work from time to time placed under my control.

(2) Not to disclose information affecting the business of the Company or their customers except in the due performance of my duties.

(3) Not to withdraw my services under any circumstances without first giving to the Company the requisite notice to terminate my engagement, viz. :— 28 days if a member of the Salaried Staff, and 7 days if a member of the Wages Staff.

SIXPENNY STAMP

Signature ....

Grade ....

Place of Employment ....

Date ....

Witness :

Signature ....

Grade ....

NOTE.—A copy of this undertaking to be given to the signatory.

The form introduced by the GWR for new supervisory staff after the Strike (there was a similar one for existing supervisors, on promotion), and a very similar form still in use on BR (WR) in 1963.

B.R. 6698

BRITISH TRANSPORT COMMISSION

BRITISH RAILWAYS (WESTERN REGION)

On appointment to the supervisory staff I, the undersigned, undertake :—

(1) To do everything within my power to promote the best interests of the Commission and efficiently to perform the work from time to time placed under my control.

(2) Not to disclose information affecting the business of the Commission or their customers except in the due performance of my duties.

(3) Not to terminate my engagement without first giving the requisite notice, *i.e.*, 4 weeks.

Witness :

Signature A. C. Button

Grade Signalman

Signature K. Endersby

Grade Signalman Spl (A)

Place of Employment Hayes & Harlington

Date August 28th 1963.

NOTE. A copy of this undertaking to be given to the signatory.

Municipal tramway committees in particular had sought to replace union members in a number of cities prior to 12th May, and were not disposed to restore them. On Merseyside, for instance, the volunteers employed . . . were retained subsequently. In Glasgow, 368 out of 5,000 tramwaymen were suspended or dismissed after the strike. In Newport 300 volunteers were kept on by the Corporation in place of members of the General & Municipal Workers whilst the Brighton Council forced the tramways' staff to leave their union, the T&GWU.

And the railways:

It was the railway directors and managers more than any other group of employers who had been responsible for the provocation which had prolonged the General Strike in many areas after 12th May. Subsequently, however, they behaved with a certain prudence or restraint.

The railway managers were atypical, perhaps even unique, in having disposed before the end of the strike the policy they planned to follow on the resumption of work.

The actions taken by the railway companies . . . on 12th May seems, however, to have differed from place to place . . . The Great Western at Cardiff was accused of cancelling entitlements earned by past service and confiscating wages owed from before the strike . . . But however phrased and delivered, these threats created the impression among railway workers that a meek return would be received in a vengeful spirit. [G.A. Phillips then describes, as we have already seen, how the massive non-return to work persuaded the companies to withdraw the proposal to 'cancel' a week's pay and exclude supervisors from the Agreement.]

Angela Tuckett in her chapter on Swindon in Jeffrey Skelley's book *The General Strike, 1926* writes:

On Monday, 10 May . . . there was a new note of anxiety and rising anger in the town, because of the latest communication from the GWR which was posted up outside the NUR rooms in Temple Street. Having described the Strike . . . as 'a deep conspiracy against the State', the circular outlined the conditions under which the Works would be re-opened. It was so worded as to be taken to mean that if and when employees were taken back, it would be as new starts, with consequent loss of seniority, pay and privileges. Moreover, they would be subject to claims for damages having broken their contract; and those in positions of special responsibility would not be taken back nor those taking a leading part in the strike.

After the Strike ended:

Straightaway they found themselves on a four-day week with all the shops closed 'until further notice' on Mondays and Saturdays. In addition they found that the GWR was blocking reinstatement. On Sunday 23rd May, several thousands met in Princess Street Recreation Ground and passed a resolution expressing 'disapproval of the spirit in which the GWR has met the settlement of the General and Railway strikes . . .'

Railway Clerks had not been reinstated according to traffic and work being found . . . In Swindon something like 80 per cent of the clerical staff had been on strike. Throughout the whole period they were under the impression that they had been dismissed by the railway company . . . and it seemed a high probability that they would not be re-employed. Other unions returned to work immediately, even though on short time; but clerical staff were kept out . . . Many didn't return for over six months . . . The bitterness against those who had stayed in was keen. When they got back to work

eventually some didn't speak to colleagues they sat next to for over a year.
Many from 'the Western' were obliged to leave Swindon, for the most part never to return.

On 21st May the railway managers and the Trade Unions again sat down to discuss the vexed question of suspension of the Guaranteed Week. In the light of the continuing Coal Strike and the general loss of traffic, it was not possible to take all the strikers back to work. It was agreed that the only fair way of sharing the available work was by suspension of the Guaranteed Week, and for work to be distributed among the men in each grade so that everyone earned the equivalent of three days pay. Similar arrangements were made for clerical and supervisory staff on 2nd June. Neither of these 'supplementary agreements' to the 14th May document applied to non-strikers who continued to be paid for a full week.

The Table in Chapter Three for the Cardiff Division shows how this worked in practice and, in the case of that division, how the percentage of staff employed rose very slowly from 59 per cent of normal in June to 89 per cent at the end of the year.

Turning now to the GWR's part in any 'victimisation', on 20th May the three unions wrote to the Secretary of the Railway Staff Conference following numerous complaints from members with regard to reinstatement. The letter summarised the complaints under five headings, giving typical cases as examples. In each case only the examples concerning the GWR are quoted here:

1. Reinstatement of Supervisors and Clerical Employees

Banbury	Supervisor and foreman not reinstated; Depot Manager refusing to meet staff.
Kingham	Station master not reinstated.
Craven Arms	Traffic inspector and chief inspector not reinstated.
Exeter	A 4th class inspector doing the work of the chief station inspector (class 3).
Penzance	Two traffic inspectors and chargeman carriage cleaner not reinstated.
Plymouth	Supervisor not reinstated and his office remained closed.
S. Lambeth	Clerical staff not reinstated. 'Officials' attitude to the men very bad.'

2. Cases of Intimidation [of Staff at work]
Only one example quoted, two members of a dredger gang at Birmingham. As a result the remainder of the gang could not resume work.

3. Continued Employment of Volunteers
Five examples given of cases where volunteers had taken the place of striking men and had been retained and the strikers not re-employed. These were at Uffington, Westbury, Banbury, Bristol and Dorchester.

4. Reinstatement of Junior Men in Preference to Seniors
There were many examples in this category: Landore, Glyn Neath, Llanelly, Abersychan & Talywain, Keynsham, Tredegar, Pontrhydyfen, Dudley, Bristol, Uffington, Abercynon, Dorchester, Exeter (77 men involved), Gloucester, Birmingham (Road Transport Dept).

5. Men Working Overtime while Others Not Reinstated
No GWR examples.

Not long after the Strike settlement on 14th May, the GWR sent the Trade Unions a list of 55 names of staff intended to be transferred to other positions without loss of pay under clause 4 of the Agreement. Heading the list was the name of the only clerk in the superintendent of the line's office to go on strike. There were 16 station masters listed: Littlemore, Kingsworthy (tellingly this man was also the Newbury NUR Branch Secretary), Corsham, Uffington, Severn Beach, Hemyock, Nancegollan, Caerphilly, Churchdown, Kingham, Tyseley, Torpantau, Afon Wen, Criccieth, Newbridge-on-Wye and Harlech. There were several inspectors listed, including the district inspector at Penzance. Most of the rest were clerks, including the chief booking clerk at Newport. The remainder were a handful of wages staff. Similar lists were sent by the other companies but the GWR's was the longest, almost half of the total names identified (117).

By 26th May the company had revised the 'Clause 4' list and it now consisted of 32 names, all of the wages grades having been removed apart from a signalman at Usk. The station masters at Severn Beach, Nancegollan, Afon Wen, Criccieth, Newbridge-on-Wye and Harlech also no longer featured; Torpantau was now on the 'Clause 5' list - *see page 107*.

At this stage the total number of names listed amongst all the companies was 94, and the three unions asked for a meeting with the companies because it had become apparent that men were being transferred to new or lower paid posts involving moving home or lodging. The meeting was held on 2nd July and the union representatives alleged that the companies were not carrying out the settlement, 'either in the letter, the spirit or the intention in which they were entered into.' With regard to clause 4, this had been accepted 'on the understanding that removals would only be made as needed, to adjust difficult cases where friction had arisen . . .' In practice, however, removals were being carried out where these circumstances did not exist and, in addition, men were being reduced in status. Examples were given of salaried inspectors reduced to wages grades, station masters to clerks or lower graded SM posts. The union leaders claimed that when clause 4 was discussed the only reference made was to transfers to other districts and not to lower positions; 'had they known any such reduction . . . was contemplated, they would not have signed the settlement.' The management representatives undertook to look into the points made.

In the *TSS Journal* (the organ of the TSSA - successor to the RCA) in May 1994, the late E.A. Wilson (then aged 92) wrote:

> I was the Correspondence Secretary of the Paddington Branch of the RCA at the time [1926]. We had one member in the Time Bill section of the Superintendent of the Line's office who came out on strike with us.
>
> When the Strike was over he was victimised by being locked out from his post, and sent to work in the station Parcel Office.
>
> I conducted a lengthy correspondence with the RCA General Secretary (Mr Walkden) who, despite his efforts, was unable to secure his reinstatement.
>
> The membership of the Paddington Branch (the largest on the GW) was around 800/900 . . . The number responding to the strike call was pathetic.
>
> I was employed in the Audit office and out of a total staff of around 200, of whom

about 50 were members, only about 12 responded and three of these defected on the first day.

When the Strike was called off . . . we reported for duty the following morning but were not allowed to resume work.

I was told that there was no work for me, but that I should report again next week on half pay. Upon doing so, I was victimised further by being sent to Kensington Addison Rd Parcel Office. In fact I did not get back to my old post in the Audit Office until some months later.

Our spirits were unbroken, though as far as the Paddington branch was concerned the Strike was a complete disaster. Our membership was decimated to some 200, and it was many years before we were able to build it up to some 1,000.

At about this time (June) the 'Paddington Railwaymen' (NUR members) published an open letter to Sir Felix Pole, expressing in very bitter terms their feelings against him personally following the collapse of the General Strike. This letter is included as Appendix Three.

On 9th August, 1926 the NUR wrote to the Acting Secretary of the TUC General Council enclosing details of members (nationwide) imprisoned, fined or refused reinstatement and asking for financial assistance with the union's costs. The list detailed 145 cases of men refused reinstatement because they had appeared at a Police court; this included 15 GWR cases. A further 26 cases (including 2 GWR) were men refused reinstatement because of charges of alleged intimidation, not yet heard in court. These details only concern NUR members, which details are archived at Warwick University.

The General Council agreed to pay on the basis of £2 per head for victimisation, £1 5*s*. 0*d*. per week for imprisonment and a part payment of fines pro-rata the size of the fine. A total sum of £679 5*s*. 0*d*. was enclosed to help the NUR.

In October 1926 there were still 45,000 NUR members unemployed and 200,000 on a 3-day week.

In September/October 1926 the NUR and RCA took a complaint to the Central Wages Board that the GWR had deferred for three months scale increments of certain members who had struck. This they contended was contrary to the Strike settlement and a breach of National agreements. The GWR's response was that such increases are dependent upon satisfactory conduct and efficient service and that 'they deemed it proper to mark their sense of admitted unsatisfactory conduct . . . by the deferment of scale increases . . .' No other company took this action.

No agreement being reached, the complaint went to the next level of the negotiating machinery, the National Wages Board on 4th January, 1927. Here the Rt Hon. J.H. Thomas PC, MP, Political Secretary of the NUR made an impassioned plea to Sir Felix Pole, who was present, before even putting the facts of the case, that, effectively, bygones should be bygones and that the parties should start 1927 by forgetting the incidents of 1926. Sir Felix responded by saying that he had offered the unions a reference to the National Wages Board last July, but they had declined. However, he was prepared to start 1927 by holding out an olive branch, though, he said, 'in parenthesis, I may say we have done it on many occasions and one is getting a little dubious as to results'.

[The parties made their cases at much greater length than set out here but I have spared the reader the wordy detail.]

Reporting the case the *Swindon Citizen* of 7th January, 1927 said:

> . . . we consider the Company's action was entirely contrary to the Strike settlement and to various National Agreements, and it is noteworthy that none of the other companies thought it permissible or desirable . . .
> . . .we suggest that Sir Felix should now go a step further and grant the customary marriage dowries which have been withheld from certain woman strikers at Swindon and elsewhere.

In 1927 a summary statement was drawn up of the action taken with men accused of violence or intimidation who had not been allowed to resume until their appeals had been heard by the General Manager (or assistant) ('clause 5 cases')*.

Post	*Charge*	*Result*
SM Torpantau	Use of language likely to cause breach of peace	Resumed 28.6.26
Driver Swindon	Intimidating and violence towards shunter	Ditto
Fireman Gloucester	Intim. and violence towards labourer	Ditto
Signalman Ardley	Breaking glass in box	Resumed 15.7.26
3 staff Penzance	Intim. volunteer bus dvr	Resumed 5 & 7.7.26
Goods guard Worcester	Unlawful speech	Resumed 21.10.26
SM Llanbrymair	Threatened replacement SM	Resumed as clerk at Builth Wells 12.7.26 (SM post abolished)
Actg Shed Chargeman Aberystwyth	(Took part in strike)	Reduced to dvr but reinstated to chargeman on appeal
C'man carr. cleaner Penzance	Intimidating inspector	Resumed 21.7.26
Shunter Swansea	Intimidating goods guard	Dismissed (this man was also a local NUR official)
Shunter Swansea	Intimidating shunter	Resumed June 1926 (brother of above)
Porter Trowbridge	Intimidating Porter	Resumed 19.12.26
Carr. cleaner Tondu	Intimidating signalman	Resumed 17.8.26
Driver Gloucester	Impeding distribution of food	Resumed 15.8.26
Fireman Aberdare	Communistic activities	Dismissed
Signalman Dorchester	Intimidating signalman	Dismissed
Signalman Highbridge	Intimidation	Resumed 12.6.26
Pcl porter Penzance	Impeding distribution of food & intimidation	Re-employed at Padd. Pcls 26.1.27
2 porters Bridgend	Inciting signalman to stop work	Resumed 31.1.27
Goods porter Paddington	Throwing stones at buses	Resumed 4.2.27
Caller-off S. Lambeth	Obstructing & assaulting police	Employed as 'new entrant' 20.5.27

*Full details including results of police prosecutions can be found in RAIL1025/224 at PRO Kew.

Post	*Charge*	*Result*
Carter Paddington	Throwing stones at buses	In April 27 offered temp. ptrs post away from London but declined
(PW) Underman Bridgend	Inciting signalman to stop work	Resumed 15.8.27

The railway companies reinstated the Guaranteed Week on 11th April, 1927.

In November 1928 a further summary was prepared of these GWR ' clause 5 cases ':

	Prosecuted	*Not Prosecuted*	*Total*
Number of men stood off under clause 5	18	11	29
Number of appeals heard by GM	15 (a)	11	26
Number appeals successful	14 (b)	9	23
Number unsuccessful	1	2	3
Number reinstated	15	9	24
Number not reinstated	3 (c)	2 (d)	5

Notes:

(a) Three men did not appeal to GM; two of these were reinstated.

(b) Includes one case (Carter, Paddington) where appeal successful but man declined re-employment.

(c) Fireman, Aberbeeg; Underman, Plymouth (not seen by GM); Carter, Paddington.

(d) Shunter, Swansea; Signalman Dorchester.

The number of GW men whose names were originally connected with charges of intimidation was 183.

So was there 'victimisation' on the GWR? That is a difficult question to answer and it can surely only be answered, authoritatively, by someone who was involved and many of them have said that there was victimisation. Certainly to those, not guilty of any violence, who were forced to take a lower paid job, or move house (at their own expense) or who did not resume work for several months, it would have seemed to be victimisation.

Other companies seem to have been just as hard. A station master on the LMS is quoted as follows in Julian Symons' book *The General Strike*:

> I and a few more men in 'responsible posts' were sacked outright, an absolutely novel and unheard-of proceeding. Others were banished to the far ends of the system, put to humiliation, lectured and reproached by the 'top bosses'. I was reinstated after dismissal, but to a very low grade job.

The GWR endorsed staff records 'Remained loyal during strike' and these entries (in red ink) were still evident in staff records in the 1950s. It must have had some effect on consideration for promotion, at least in pre-war days.

Chapter Nine

Personal Memories and Strike Miscellanea

Personal Memories

Mr T.J. Morris writes of his father's experience:

In October 1925 my father was promoted from station master, Cirencester to a similar position at Bilson Jn. At Cirencester the revenues were derived chiefly from passenger traffic, but Bilson was in the heart of the Forest of Dean and the main income came from the conveyance of coal. Indeed at Bilson little, if any, provision was made for passengers. Those such as there were used the nearby terminal station of Cinderford.

Bilson Jn virtually consisted of a huge marshalling yard into which flowed the output of the coal mines at the nearby collieries of Foxes Bridge, Crump Meadow and Lightmoor. In earlier days other collieries had existed along the adjacent Churchway branch which also used Bilson Jn as the outlet to the main line. My father had only just about settled down to his new duties when all railway movement was disrupted by the General Strike.

At Bilson there was little, if any, movement as the great collieries were also shut down. These were very dark and hungry days for the whole community. The schools in the area became veritable soup kitchens, and for a few weeks the situation remained very grave.

During the school holidays I saw a group of men approaching the railway bridge at Bilson. I quickly recognised that they were all colliers from the strike-ridden pits and I immediately became aware that they were very cross about something. Here I should explain that whilst many railwaymen, especially those in the operating grades were on strike, my father had carried on working. His office was in the middle of the marshalling yard close to the bridge on which I was sitting. He was not unsympathetic to the cause of the miners, but I was one of ten children and it never occurred to him but that he must continue working to sustain his very large family.

I watched anxiously as the picket strode down the railway lines and approached my father's office. On arrival they were met by my father's clerk - a Mr Stan Freeman - and although I could not hear what was being said it soon became evident that a fierce argument was in progress. It was at this point that the office door opened and out came my father who, for reasons of his own, had decided to don his station master's hat. He then advanced towards the group and, in what seemed no time at all, they all began to disperse. Thus an ugly situation was averted and for the first and only time at Bilson Jn I saw my father wearing his official uniform hat.

He himself told me very little about what had transpired, but the miners had clearly demanded that both my father and his clerk should cease working and this they had declined to do.

Mr Morris's wife, Mrs K.G. Morris, also has her own strike memories:

My memories of the General Strike are extremely vivid. My father was a ticket collector on the GWR at St James station, Cheltenham. My mother had just been told she had a heart condition caused by rheumatism and it would last 10 years, when she would recover. My sister was just three years old and I was seven.

I knew something was worrying my parents in addition to my mother's illness, but knew not what.

I so well remember my father coming home from work one day. He came up to the bedroom where we were sitting with mother; he was very upset and said to my mother, 'They called me "scum" when I went in to work today and my cousin was in the picket line trying to stop me going in. I cannot possibly strike with you so ill, we need the money. But it really is an awful business.' It was the first time I saw my father cry!

I certainly did not understand the Strike. I could not understand how people could be so unkind to my father when I knew how worried he was about my mother's health. However, they did not change him. The text at his funeral service was, 'He went about doing good.' Would that there were more like him.

Mr Fred Cole of Worcester, who was in his first year of school at the time, remembers this snippet:

My father was shed foreman at a small shed called Branches Fork, a sub depot of Pontypool Road, serving a number of collieries north of Pontypool. After the Strike was declared he remained loyal for a few days, but with no staff booking on duty, he was persuaded to join the strikers. To ensure the safety of the depot he locked all doors, and secured everything moveable in the yard. That same evening two Police officers called at home threatening to prosecute father for having in his possession property belonging to the GWR. Meaning the keys, of which they took possession.

He stayed out until the Strike ended, but before being allowed to resume duty he was summoned to attend at the divisional office, Newport, where he was seen by the locomotive superintendent and told in no uncertain manner that when a person is appointed to a position of trust, absolute loyalty was expected of them.

Mr J. Harber of Swindon recalls:

My father was a fitter in the Loco Works and also a part time fireman of the Works Brigade. The AEU allowed him to attend fires and emergencies.

I was 10 years old in 1926 and lived in the railway estate. Most of the Strike activities took place around the estate. The Strike meetings were held in the park and the picketing took place at the main entrance.

As the estate and park were private property, any strike activity was trespassing. W. Robins and W. Noble, who were Secretary RCA and District Secretary AEU, were arrested for trespassing during a picket.

The Revd K. Crisford, who was a curate at St Mark's, preached a sermon against the railway companies and the Government and supported the strikers. After the service he walked to the park in his cassock and surplice with supporting parishioners to address a Strike meeting.

This was not supported by all the church members; some who were managers, foremen and 'hopefuls' shifted their allegiance to Christ Church. [After the Strike the Revd Mr Crisford was forced to leave Swindon.]

On a more personal note our school swimming lessons were stopped due to the water being supplied from the Loco Works, and the boilermen being on strike.

Mr R.L. Bull of Windsor was an undergraduate of University College, London at the time. He writes as follows:

I lived at home (Windsor) and commuted to college. The Strike happened just a few weeks before my Finals, so for the first half of the Strike I stayed with a friend nearer London.

But for the second half I managed to travel to and from Windsor. One train from Windsor ran through to Paddington stopping up to West Drayton and then running non-stop to Paddington. It left at 8.12 am. As this train had to carry passengers normally on several trains, it was fairly full on leaving Windsor and you can imagine how full it was by the time it left West Drayton.

I remember coming home once from Paddington and it had been decided that the train would stop at Iver. Although Iver station opened in December 1924, there was, in May 1926, no down main platform. The train I was on ran on the down main and stopped at Iver by a grassy bank. The passengers who wished to alight had to jump down as best they could.

The normal running time between Slough and Windsor was seven minutes and it was said at the time that one of the Strike drivers did it in five and a half minutes. I cannot vouch for this, but I do remember that the curve between Windsor River Bridge and Windsor station was taken pretty smartly.

A Fishguard Harbour Incident

(From the *County Echo* (Fishguard) 13th May, 1926)

I am a retired railway servant, and I offered my services to the station master at Fishguard Harbour to help unload foodstuff from ships at the harbour. I worked Friday, Saturday and Sunday, but on Saturday night I had a letter brought to me from the strike committee, strongly complaining about me working at the Harbour and calling me a 'blackleg' and also saying I should remember past favours of the staff at the Harbour. Now Mr Editor I don't mind their calling me a 'blackleg.' That hurts no man. But what I strongly complain about is the past favours which were all given voluntarily. The favour conferred on myself was when I retired I received a presentation walking stick and a wallet containing money (£11 5*s*.). The favour conferred on my late son during his illness was an allowance of £24 17*s*. All this I am returning to the strike committee to pay back the men that gave it, for I consider that no one can insult a mother and father more than by throwing up to them what they did for their son who is dead. (The writer was a retired inspector from the Traffic Department.)

Loss of Privileges

The following circular was issued by the CME's Department at Swindon on 5th May, 1926, but was probably a standard instruction issued throughout the company.

Will you please note that during the period of the Strike passes must only be issued for Company's business.
Privilege tickets may be issued to members of the loyal staff in cases of emergency only, such as serious illness, or death in family, *but on no account to those on strike.*

'Secret' Instructions to Station Masters

The following paragraphs are abbreviated extracts from a 'Secret' document issued by the divisional superintendent, Birmingham on 3rd May, 1926. It was headed:' Notes of General Principles for Guidance of Station Masters, but who will be Required to Use Discretion and Act Largely in Accordance with Local Circumstances, in the Event of a Railway Strike.'

Get in touch with Police Authorities for protection of loyal workers, volunteers and their families and vulnerable points if really necessary, or if strikers intimidate workers . . .

Cease the acceptance and forwarding of all Passenger, Parcels and Goods traffic . . . unless it can be ascertained that a service can be given.

Cease loading all foodstuffs and perishable traffic . . . unless it can be ascertained . . . [as before].

Perishable and food traffic already loaded should not be despatched . . . and the owners requested . . . to cart it away . . . unless it can be ascertained . . . [as before].

Milk traffic must be given the first consideration and any available power must be used for this traffic.

Advise divisional superintendent and district goods manager immediately of all foodstuffs and perishables in the company's possession . . . also what petrol tank wagons are on hand . . .

Arrangements [must be] made to prevent long hours as far as possible to workers by introducing early a roster working.

Complete and prompt reports to be made to the divisional superintendent of [abandoned trains]:

(a) Where and at what time train left (say if within station limits or not)
(b) Condition of engine, i.e. whether fire drawn or boiler empty
(c) Names of trainmen concerned and home station
(d) If goods train, number of wagons and contents
(e) Present position of train

Complete and prompt reports to be made . . . of:
(1) Signal boxes left in circumstances calculated to involve danger to the public
(2) Damage to property
(3) Intimidation
(4) Illegal picketing

Anyone caught deliberately causing damage to the railway . . . or assaulting or otherwise molesting loyal servants to be given in charge [i.e. handed over to the authorities].

The following lines and places will be protected by the company's police:

Banbury LN&E Jn to Banbury station including Passenger, Goods and Locomotive Depots

Tyseley to Shrewsbury end of Oxley Sidings including all Depots

Stourbridge Jn to Town Goods Yard, Locomotive and Town stations

. . . Local banking [of money] may be resorted to . . .

If difficulty arises owing to shortage of money for wages etc., the Chief Accountant should be communicated with . . .

A Station Master's Viewpoint

A loyal station master at Smethwick Jn, Mr Cripps, wrote to the Birmingham superintendent on 10th May:

I am keeping in touch with all stations each side of me continuously.

All traffic received here has been cleared. Position up to present quiet but the station is well picketed on all sides and my movements watched with interest. They have been trying to get hold of my junior clerk but so far we have been able to thwart them.

We have a quantity of relaying material scattered about the line here, very useful to do damage, but having in mind the disturbances of 1911, I am taking precautions to inspect line, each side of station personally at 7 am, during the day, and between 8 and 10 pm each night.

With regard to the pensioners to whom letters have been sent, I have seen pensioners (signalmen) Bailey and Webb, but both are too old and shaky to be of service . . .

Our passengers, especially the large number of Season Ticket holders, are appreciating the service run and are making good use of this.

I can only hope that all possible can be done to defeat this Strike . . . and for the country to come out victorious and assist the Government and Companies, to which end I am prepared . . . to open the signal box to assist the traffic, or any other duties required.

Notice to Engine Drivers

The following undated notice was issued by the Birmingham superintendent:

Advise drivers of all trains starting from your station [Wolverhampton, Stourbridge Jn, Knowle, Birmingham, Acocks Green] commencing tomorrow that a number of signal boxes are closed and the signals left at alright, and that Stop signals at danger must be observed and not passed without special authority.

The Down Starting signal at Swan Village North and the Up Starting signal at Priestfield Jn cannot be lowered so long as the box is closed.

West Country Happenings

The Torbay *Herald & Express* by keeping in touch with the station masters at Torre and Torquay was able to provide some interesting reports of local happenings, as follows:

Tuesday 4th May

At Torre station about half a dozen men [presumably strikers] arrived at 6 am and, having secured a substantial supply of Woodbines, proceeded to indulge in a little physical recreation by playing football in the station yard. At 7 am Mr West the station master put in an appearance and the clerks on duty also arrived. All signals were down but there was no one on duty at the station, or in the goods sheds, with the exception of the clerks. At Torquay the situation was very similar, only the station master and the clerks put in an appearance.

Wednesday 5th May

Mr West informed our reporter that Torquay supplies were being fetched from Newton Abbot by road vehicles and he could see from the constant stream of vehicles which passed . . . this arrangement was working most satisfactorily [!]

Thursday 6th May

GWR ran a bus for season ticket holders between Paignton and Dartmouth . . . leaving Paignton at 7.30 am and 5.30 pm.

Saturday 8th May

Mr West advises that all the towns on the Torquay branch are kept in touch with Newton Abbot by the bus service in a very satisfactory manner [!]

Sunday 9th May
Five trains each way over the Torquay branch (first since the Strike started).

Tuesday 11th May
Four trains each way over the Brixham branch (first since Strike started).

Thursday 13th May
An empty fish van derailed at Churston in the evening. Trains could only use one platform.

Saturday 15th May
All the staff at Torre reported for duty and two signalmen and one carman have returned to work. Others will be taken back as train service is improved . . . At Torquay the station master hopes that some of the men will be re-employed on Monday. At Totnes whole staff reported but not necessary to add to the present staff. No additional staff taken on at Paignton and at Newton Abbot about 12 men in the Traffic Dept taken on.

Another interesting report in the *Herald & Express* concerned an Anglican priest at Brixham who, it seems, had taken very readily to engine driving:

Reverend G. Gordon, priest-in-charge at St Peter's Church, Brixham, was one of the volunteers who did service on the locomotives in the West of England during the strike. He commenced duty at Newton Abbot on Wednesday 12th and was put on one of the passenger trains between Newton Abbot and Taunton as a supplementary driver to learn the road to Taunton. On Thursday and Friday he took entire charge of an engine at Newton Abbot and was engaged in shunting operations there each day from 9 am to 7 pm. On Saturday he was on the leading engine between Newton Abbot and Plymouth.

On Thursday (Ascension Day) before going to Newton Abbot he officiated at a fully choral Holy Communion at St Peter's. Mr Gordon had previous experience as an engine driver through his six years association with the engineering firm of Kitson's at Leeds.

'It is not by any means an easy task for any amateur fireman to find the firehole door with coal when the engine is rocking about at full speed', said Mr Gordon. 'I feel that the general public do not sufficiently recognise the "black squad" on duty at the front of the train', emphasised Mr Gordon.

The *Western Times* in its 21st May edition recorded an amateur operation on the Culm Valley line (Hemyock branch) which had begun on 14th May, and been very well received by the 'locals'. Both driver and fireman were 'public school men':

Welcome was far more enthusiastic than that of the Exe Valley. People cheered us all the way along the line and stations were crowded to give us a hearty greeting. At Culmstock the local JP turned out and congratulated us . . . The guards were regular servants who had remained loyal.

With a full load out of Tiverton Jn we experienced no difficulty ascending the steep bank outside the station - the driver on this occasion was Mr Allen, the pilot driver Mr Russell, loco foreman at Exeter and Mr Kenrick-Welby, of Wimbledon, the fireman.

On the Tavistock branch in Devon a former captain of Plymouth Argyle FC,

J.C. Pethick, drove the only train on the branch from Monday 10th May onwards. When the *Western Morning News* reporter joined him on the footplate on 15th May, Mr Pethick was being assisted by *two* staff firemen who had struck for two days but then returned to work. Mr Pethick's only previous experience had been with contractors' locomotives. On his first day on the branch he had worked from 6 am to 8.30 pm, but afterwards this had settled down to 12 hour days (presumably the reason for needing two firemen).

Goods Traffic at Newbury

The *Newbury Weekly News* of 13th May has an interesting account of goods traffic received at Newbury during the Strike, something not much reported upon generally:

4th May	21 trucks coal (16 for gas works), 3 tarmac, 2 coke, 24 miscellaneous goods
7th May	1 truck coal, 2 miscellaneous goods
10th May	7 trucks coal, 7 tarmac, 5 miscellaneous
11th May	12 trucks coal, 1 coke, 2 miscellaneous

During the Strike a dozen or fifteen trucks of goods, mostly foodstuffs, have been unloaded on the deck and across the main line for local distribution. On Monday (10th May), Tuesday and yesterday trucks containing margarine, butter, eggs etc. and general foodstuffs arrived and were speedily unloaded. The train abandoned at the Racecourse station on the day the Strike began, included trucks loaded with eggs and cabbage. Some of these were taken on to London. The cabbage was taken delivery of by the consignees from London who sent down two lorries to fetch it.

Appendix One

Brief Diary of National Events

Friday 30th April

Government subsidy to the coal owners ceases. The coal owners impose new terms, effectively locking the miners out.

Saturday 1st May

General Council of TUC announces General Strike to commence at midnight 3rd May if the coal crisis has not been settled by then.

Government declares State of Emergency.

Sunday 2nd May

Negotiations commence at 9 pm but are broken off at 1 am (Monday) after Government claims interference with the Press (*Daily Mail* printers had refused to print a leading article denouncing the Strike).

Monday 3rd May

Government will not resume negotiations without unconditional withdrawal of Strike threat.

General Strike starts at midnight (Mon./Tues.)

Tuesday 4th May

Stoppage fairly complete. Hardly any trains, buses or trams. Docks closed. No national newspapers.

Wednesday 5th May

Government appeals for volunteers.

Government issues the *British Gazette* newspaper (ed. Winston Churchill) from *Morning Post* premises.

Thursday 6th May

Government assures strikers who return to work that it will prevent them being victimised.

Sir John Simon, Home Secretary in Asquith's War Cabinet and an eminent lawyer, declares the Strike illegal, in the House of Commons.

Friday 7th May

The Archbishop of Canterbury puts forward proposals for a settlement. This information is suppressed by the *British Gazette* and the BBC.

Saturday 8th May

Government decides to recruit a Civil Reserve Constabulary, equipped with steel helmets and truncheons, to supplement the Police and Special Constabulary. To be recruited from the TA and ex-military men.

Food supplies convoyed to Hyde Park with armoured car escort.

Sunday 9th May

Roman Catholic Cardinal denounces the Strike as a sin.

Monday 10th May
Sir Herbert Samuel meets TUC and miners' representatives on an unofficial basis. The miners say they cannot accept wage cuts.
The BBC announces many arrests. The TUC says 'Stand firm'.

Tuesday 11th May
Mr Justice Astbury states in a judgement that the Strike is illegal 'and those inciting persons to it were not protected by the Trades Disputes Act.'
The TUC General Council accepts the final draft of the Samuel memorandum, but the miners turn it down because it involves wage cuts. ['That settled the matter for us. We had fought for them, but when it came to a show-down they turned away from us. We felt that nothing would satisfy them, and decided to call off the Strike!' - J.H. Thomas]

Wednesday 12th May
The General Strike called off unconditionally at noon. In the evening the King broadcasts a message urging co-operation and to forget bitterness. The Prime Minister in the House asks that all malice and vindictiveness 'should be put behind us.'
In the end less than a tenth of the half-million volunteers who enrolled were actually used during the Strike.

Thursday 13th May
Miners' strike continues. Railwaymen and many others refuse to return to work because of employers' unacceptable terms of reinstatement.

Friday 14th May
PM Stanley Baldwin sends terms to miners (and coal owners) even less favourable than the Samuel memorandum which the miners had rejected.
Railway unions accept terms for a return to work.

15th-18th May
General resumption of work, where work is available; the miners stay out.

20th May
Miners reject Baldwin's terms of 14th May.

end-November
Miners' strike finally ends.

Appendix Two

Brief Diary of GWR Events*

Monday 3rd May

GWR gave assurance that milk and perishable traffic would be given priority.

United Dairies had 1,100 lorries available if milk trains did not run.

Paddington Goods Local Departmental Committee (local union body) to be asked whether they will handle perishables.

Material by the lineside to be watched during the Strike.

STRIKE STARTED AT MIDNIGHT.

Tuesday 4th May

86.4 per cent of wages staff and 23.5 per cent clerical/supervisory staff on strike.

So many of the clerical staff on strike declared to be a new feature.

Some cream and fish on hand at Cardiff for the north had to be sold locally as it could not be moved.

Naval ratings working Park Royal generating station, sleeping in the station waiting room.

Services between Reading and Bramley Depot arranged for 300 workmen.

Two boatloads of potatoes from France arrived at Plymouth.

38 passengers who arrived at Fishguard on the Cork boat remained on board; the remainder went forward by road.

100 volunteers on duty at Paddington station; arrangements in hand to man several signal boxes with volunteers.

The Navy offered engineers to drive engines in the Plymouth area.

A petrol engine sent from Park Royal to Paddington Goods for shunting purposes.

Wednesday 5th May

Train services in the Chester division supplemented by road motors.

Large consignments of food accepted in Plymouth division; local traffic cleared by road.

41 wagons unloaded at Slough and delivered by Eton College boys.

At Kensington Addison Road clerical staff subjected to annoyance when going to and from their meals and arrangements made to take food to them.

Station master at Llanfynydd intimidated by the colliers when *en route* to Brymbo with revenue cash.

R.V. Payne of Reading offered use of his vehicles and staff without charge to deliver parcels at Reading; offer accepted.

Swansea Telegraph Office re-opened by clerks sent from Paddington.

Petrol engine used at Reading Goods for shunting purposes.

Road motor service at Corwen provided by a leading porter at Rossett who volunteered to do the work.

Police protection given to men working on *SS Reindeer* in Jersey, and to traders' teams delivering traffic in the Wolverhampton area.

194 passenger, milk and perishables trains run in 24 hours to 9 pm.

No trains ran on the following 'important' lines: Paddington-Banbury via Bicester Worcester-Stourbridge Jn-Wolverhampton; North Warwick line west of Henley-in-Arden; Cardiff and West Wales except for one fish train.

The following signal boxes open in the London division:

---

* This Appendix excludes events already recorded in the SOL log (see Chapter 2).

Paddington Arrival
Paddington Departure
Westbourne Bridge
Subway Junction
Portobello
West London Ground Frame
Old Oak Common East
Old Oak Common West
Acton East
Ealing
West Ealing
Hanwell East
Southall East Station
Southall West Station
West Drayton West
Slough East
Slough Middle
Taplow East
Greenford East
Northolt Jcn East
Ruislip
High Wycombe South
Saunderton
Maidenhead West
Maidenhead Middle
Waltham Sidings
Shottesbrook
Ruscombe
Twyford East
Twyford West
Kennet Bridge
Reading East Main
Reading West Main
Tilehurst
Pangbourne
Goring
Didcot East Jcn
Didcot East End
Didcot West End
Foxhall Jcn
Milton
Didcot North
Appleford Crossing
Culham
Radley
Abingdon
Oxford Goods Shed
Oxford Engine Shed
Wolvercot Jcn
Yarnton Jcn
Basingstoke
Colthrop Crossing
Newbury Middle
Hampstead Crossing
Kintbury
Hungerford West
Woodhay
Burghclere
Litchfield
King's Worthy

Thursday 6th May

A special train run from Portishead to Handsworth with petrol.

Special train Didcot Camp to Paddington with 100 tons camp equipment for RAOC: War Office pleased.

Letter received by station master Kensington from NUR demanding that he cease work; he remained at work.

GWR motor lorry conveyed goods from Ruabon to Cefn and Barmouth.

GWR van stopped by strikers in the Birmingham area - police protection obtained.

175 volunteers at Paddington station; 26 additional signal boxes opened in London division making 86 in total.

Kingsbridge branch re-opened and Saltash railmotor extended to Plympton, both using volunteers.

Retired workers used in Worcester and Birmingham districts.

Paddington Enquiry Office to remain open continuously.

Horsehay Co. offered their engine to work between Horsehay and Wellington, but not taken up.

Barry Dock telephone exchange re-opened.

Birkenhead-Liverpool ferry operating full service.

79 drivers on duty - CME asked to ensure best use made of their services.

Two lorries at Battersea interfered with and put out of action temporarily.

957 volunteers employed (London, Bristol, West of England), 129 volunteers in South Wales and 225 in the Midlands and Northern area.

At Cardiff six potato boats being unloaded by volunteers.

355 passenger, milk and perishable trains run in 24 hours to 9 pm.

No service on the following 'important' lines:

Paddington-Banbury via Bicester

North Warwick line west of Henley-in-Arden

West Wales, west of Swansea

Friday 7th May

Plea from men not on strike at Reading Signal Works to be 'locked out' because of threats by strikers; this was declined and police protection would be asked for.

All privilege tickets to be suspended and free passes only to be issued on company's business.

No overtime, night or Sunday pay to be paid to volunteers.

AGM J. Milne asked to look into possible future suspension of work because of the Strike.

100 boxes of fish sent from Cardiff to Paddington by ordinary train.

Strikers at Southall attempted to stop a guard booking on.

87 signal boxes open in London division.

Signal wires cut at Penarth and Grangetown and permanent way keys removed between Acton and Ealing.

Volunteers at work: 981 (London-West of England), 252 South Wales and 344 Midlands & North

300 passengers from two liners landed at Plymouth, baggage handled by volunteers; Shipping Agents 'greatly satisfied'.

479 passenger etc. trains run in 24 hours to 9 pm. Lines with no service, as before.

Saturday 8th May

No shunters on duty in the Swansea division.

A further case of interference with signal wires at Penarth.

A shunter at Snow Hill allowed to remain on premises after receiving threats.

160 volunteers presented themselves at Plymouth yesterday (Friday). Many will be trained as shunters.

Goods train run South Wales-Paddington with 10 trucks of cattle and 16 general merchandise.

A train of Government stores Didcot-Paddington arranged.

Several firms offering their enginemen to assist.

Agreed clerks could become special constables if their normal work could be suspended.

50 per cent of London division signal boxes open.

612 passenger etc. trains run in 24 hours to 9 pm.

Important lines with no service:

Paddington-Banbury via Bicester

Henley-in-Arden - Honeybourne

Cheltenham-Bristol

Swansea-Carmarthen

Clarbeston Road-Fishguard

Sunday 9th May

No shunters in Swansea division.

Expected to open tomorrow (Monday):

Carmarthen-Aberystwyth
Pembroke-Tenby / Whitland
Falmouth branch
Helston branch
St Ives branch
Tavistock branch
Barnstaple branch
Moretonhampstead branch
Tiverton branch
Dulverton branch
Clevedon branch
Newcastle Emlyn branch
Cardigan branch
Milford Haven branch
Fishguard-Clarbeston Rd
Festiniog branch

184 passengers from three liners conveyed from Plymouth to Paddington.

Stones thrown near Westbourne Park station and at Upper Pontnewydd.

Strikers caused disturbance at Little Mill Jn; strikers tried to persuade Abersychan (Low Level) SM to undertake only normal duties, which he declined; station masters at Dowlais pressed to strike by large crowd; station master at Cockett accused of 'black-legging'; inspector at Llanelly Dock visited at his home and threatened - police protection provided.

Henley-in-Arden SM visited by *striking* SMs from Tyseley (GW) and Hednesford (LMS) who tried to persuade him to strike.

175 volunteers working at Paddington station.

492 passenger etc. trains run in 24 hours to 9 pm.

Important lines with no service, as before plus Chester-Birkenhead and Chester-Manchester (Exchange).

Monday 10th May

Freight trains run over Windsor, Fairford, Wycombe, Calne, Ledbury and Aberystwyth branches.

New services between:

Cholsey-Wallingford
Oxford-Blenheim
Eastern Valleys
Worcester-Honeybourne
Stratford-Leamington

Additional trips run on Staines, Uxbridge, Windsor and Abingdon branches.

Bridport, Brixham and Looe branches to re-open 11th May, also Swansea-Glyn Neath.

'Fish, milk, cheese, cream, butter, eggs and other foodstuffs have been freely accepted in this area [London, Bristol and W of England] and considerable quantities have been conveyed by passenger trains, supplemented in some cases by freight trains. The destinations included Cardiff, Glasgow and Bradford, and large consignments have passed between the W of England and various points *en route* to London.'

A special left Plymouth Docks at 1.47 pm with 350 'Ocean' passengers for Paddington. First train from Docks station, rather than Millbay.

Three would-be saboteurs carrying wire cutters discovered at Northolt Jn.

455 volunteers on duty at Paddington station.

99 signal boxes now open in London division. 48 signal boxes open in Swansea division and more expected to open tomorrow (Tuesday).

A 10-minute service being run between Ealing and Shepherds Bush.

3,000 public inquiries at Paddington between 9 am and 6 pm.

Volunteers employed: 1,038 (London, Bristol and W of England), 487 (S. Wales) and 720 (Midlands & North).

908 passenger etc. trains in 24 hours to 9 pm.

Lines with no service as before, except Clarbeston Rd-Fishguard and Chester-Birkenhead now had trains.

Tuesday 11th May

270 sets enginemen available throughout GWR (Monday) and 316 sets today. (In the end was 357 sets.)

79 consulting engineers offered their services to the locomotive department at Cardiff.

A team of Headquarters' officials, called 'Co-ordinating Officers' appointed, one to each division, to assist local officers in the tricky business of deciding how many men will be required for work when the Strike ended.

212 inwards and 171 outwards wagons dealt with at Oxley.

From the start of the Strike up to 7 am 11th May, 538 traffic dept wages grade strikers had asked to return to work of whom 406 were reinstated.

New services put on Aylesbury-High Wycombe, Oxford-Thame, Honeybourne-Stratford, and extension of the Bewdley-Tenbury Wells service to Woofferton.

Anticipated new services tomorrow (Wednesday): Newport-Rogerstone, Newport-Machen. Also engines expected to be available at Severn Tunnel Jn and Pontypool Road for the first time.

474 volunteers on duty at Paddington station. 253 volunteers enrolled in Exeter division of whom 112 employed.

118 signal boxes (London) and 56 (Swansea) now open.

1,022 passengers etc. trains run in 24 hours to 9 pm.

Important lines with no service now:

Paddington-Banbury via Bicester
Swansea-Carmarthen
Cheltenham-Bristol
Warrington-Manchester (Exchange)

Wednesday 12th May

Re yesterday's report, actually 50 consulting engineers offered their services of which 14 were working, 10 were training and the rest 'standing by'.

All applications for coal and firewood (which the company normally supplied at 'privileged' rates) by strikers were regarded as cancelled.

Intended to run a 50 per cent service tomorrow and as full a goods service as possible.

Locomotive, etc. Works not to re-open until Monday.

Chester-Manchester (Exch.) service run (previously terminated Warrington). Other lines shown closed yesterday remained closed.

Helsby branch re-opened.

Three special trains conveying 'Ocean' passengers, baggage and mails run from Plymouth Docks to Paddington.

Large consignments of flour carried from Gloucester, Avonmouth and Cardiff; cattle traffic accepted at Hereford, Leamington and Oswestry.

1,170 passenger etc. trains run in 24 hours to 9 pm.

Thursday 13th May

381 sets of enginemen available, Wednesday.

There is to be no general disbandment of volunteers or special constables yet.

Not able to introduce the increased passenger service hoped for yesterday.

Four complete trains of vegetables run from the Worcester district.

Derailment in Southall yard prevented some margarine traffic going forward.

500 volunteers on duty at Paddington station. 321 volunteers enrolled in Exeter division of whom 128 employed (one suspects that this is a cumulative figure since the Strike started).

SS *Sambur* conveyed 28,303 packages of produce Guernsey-Weymouth; SS *Reindeer* 2,905 packages and 62 tons potatoes between the same places.

Friday 14th May

Terms of settlement (Railway Strike) agreed.

Intend to run a 50 per cent passenger service on Monday.

Intend to run first trains between Swansea and Carmarthen today.

West London line signal boxes open.

Three drivers and firemen from Brymbo Steel Works usefully employed in Chester division.

500 volunteers at Paddington station.

Friday 21st May

Loyal staff will be allowed to take annual leave in the usual way; the arrangements for other staff to be decided later.

Privilege tickets restored to staff at Swindon Works; the question of other staff was deferred. [No explanation is given for this decision.]

The report of the Committee appointed to review the arrangements for rewarding loyal staff and volunteers was tabled.

The British Gazette

Published by His Majesty's Stationery Office.

No. 8 — LONDON, THURSDAY, MAY 13, 1926. — ONE PENNY.

GENERAL STRIKE OFF

UNCONDITIONAL WITHDRAWAL OF NOTICES BY T.U.C.

Men To Return Forthwith.

SURRENDER RECEIVED BY PREMIER IN DOWNING STREET.

Negotiations To Be Resumed In The Coal Dispute.

The General Strike, which began at midnight on Monday, May 3, ended yesterday in an unconditional withdrawal of the strike notices by the General Council of the Trades Union Congress. The news of the settlement was conveyed to the public in the following official communiqué :—

WHITEHALL, May 12.

It was intimated to the Prime Minister that the Trades Union Council desired to come and see him at Downing-street, and they arrived soon after 12 noon. Mr. Pugh made a statement, in which he stated that the Trades Union Council had decided to call off the strike notices forthwith.

The Prime Minister then spoke briefly. He stated that he was very glad to hear what Mr. Pugh had said, and he would report it to his colleagues in the Cabinet.

As regards the coal industry, the Prime Minister said that negotiations would be resumed, and the Government would consider as to what steps should be taken.

The whole proceedings lasted a very few minutes.

THE DECISION OF THE T.U.C.

NO RESUMPTION BY MINERS.

Mr. Cook And End Of The General Strike.

"Nothing To Do With Us."

THE KING TO THE NATION.

Appeal For Lasting Peace.

DIFFICULTIES STILL AHEAD.

"Let Us Forget Elements of Bitterness."

TO MY PEOPLE.

REINSTATEMENT.

No Obligations Incurred.

CIVIL SERVICE.

Home Secretary And Volunteer Labour.

POSTAL SERVICES.

Delivery Of Parcels To Be Resumed.

VOLUNTARY SERVICES.

APRIL TRADE RESULTS.

MR. BALDWIN ON THE FINISH.

Victory Of Common Sense.

STATEMENT IN PARLIAMENT.

NATURE OF THE PEACE.

THE NEWS IN PARIS.

Profound Belief In British Circles.

RESUMPTION OF RACING.

THE BIRTH AND LIFE OF THE "BRITISH GAZETTE"

An Unexampled Achievement In Journalism.

HOW AN IMPROVISED NEWSPAPER REACHED A CIRCULATION OF 2,209,000.

THE GOVERNMENT ARRIVES.

A FAMOUS LETTER.

(Continued on Page 2.)

"British Gazette" Circulation.

May 5	232,000
May 6	507,000
May 7	655,000
May 8	836,000
May 10	1,127,600
May 11	1,801,400
May 12	2,209,000

The Morning Post.

ON FRIDAY, MAY 14, THE MORNING POST will RESUME PUBLICATION.

Price ONE Penny

The Cover of *The British Gazette* (ed. W.S. Churchill) for 13th May, 1926 announcing the end of the Strike.

Appendix Three

Open Letter to Sir Felix Pole from the Paddington Railwaymen

From **The Paddington Railwaymen**
June 1926

Sir,

The chief feature of your career as General Manager has been that which has appealed to the staff of the Great Western Railway for co-operation; urging that such was in the best interests of the men, the public and the Company.

The men for a number of years have believed you, and have been prepared to accept your advice. They have watched your movements, and for a period believed that at last they had an open and fair-minded official to deal with. Even up to the end of April they held this opinion, but even you, must recognise that, while not receiving the education to which they were entitled, they are not void of every atom of intelligence, as may be desired by the shareholding class whom you represent in the railway industry. **We like you, recognise the class struggle** which is being waged in Society, and again we recognise that if we are to resist the attacks of your class, **we also, like you, must be organised as a class:** i.e. under a single central leadership.

Having decided on this as a mass body of workers we placed our leadership in the General Council of the Trades Union Congress, and they, acting upon instructions of our Executive Committees decided that the time had arrived when the miners must be protected from the onslaught of your profit-grabbing class. It was here that you gave us a real demonstration of your co-operative spirit. You asked us to ignore our mining comrades; to let them fight a lone battle, while we, in our turn, should stand by and see them starved into accepting the conditions your class wished to force upon them. Your circulars and pleadings, your vomitations and cries left us cold; we thought first of the "old Company," then you, and then our mining comrades, and finally decided our first duty was to our class and not to our enemies. Therefore, on the morning of May the 4th, you were left in your true position to line up **with** the Federation of British Industries **against the workers.**

There is one thing we want to know. If, as you have said so often, you believed in co-operation, with decent conditions for all, why did you not join hands with that section which was attempting to carry this into effect? Why did you not point out to the mineowners that they had no right to make huge profits; live lives of gorgeous luxury; to sneer at all wage earners, and at the same time attempt to force those who had produced that profit still further down into the mire of misery and poverty? Why did you not attack the mineowners? Because they belonged to the same greedy dividend-drawing class as you, and **we realise here that your pleas for co-operation have been to much hypocritical trash.** This you have proved since the termination of the General Strike. The agreement arrived at smells of you throughout. So you think you have "got your own back" — we shall see. The June issue of the Great Western Railway magazine shows the shadow of "Poleism" right through. We advise all railwaymen not to buy your anti-working class propaganda doping magazine.

Your victimising attitude since the strike shows how you intend to penalise our men. Again we say, "We shall see." We have seen you at last in your true colours. We see you arraigned as one of the biggest advocates of Capitalism that we have ever witnessed. We see you as an advocate of further suffering for our class. But we in our turn stand solid, **yes, as solidly as on May 4th,** and we say to you now that we know where we are, we shall continue to fight you and your class. Not only the mines, but the railways as well must be wrested from private enterprise.

Even though the General Strike has finished, our thoughts still go out to the miners. We shall still support them or any other workers whenever we think fit. But there is one thing we cannot do, and that is in reference to your recent circular letter telling us that unless we speak to the "scabs" we are liable to dismissal. No man who sells his soul and his self respect to his enemies and betrays his comrades is entitled to the companionship of a class-conscious worker and we ignore your circular. It may be advisable from your point of view to post notices and agreements, but we men have yet to see the purpose, except as an insult to us, of posting them deliberately on view to the general public.

We invite you to examine the temperament of every individual who was loyal (sic) to the company, and we challenge you to pick out a real man amongst them. For, given a big enough bribe, they would sell even you to-morrow, just as you, at the bidding of a bigger salary would leave the "dear old Company" to fare for itself. Again, while your wages exceed the combined weekly wage of over fifty of our men you say the wages of the men must be reduced, and **yours** must be increased. We want to know on whose suggestion, and on what qualifications yours has been increased. One last word, dear Sir Felix, before we leave you to carry on the fight - a General Manager can leave the railway company for three months, and take a trip to the other side of the world, and no substitute need be found for him, but if through ill-health, death or even strikes, one of the cogs in the wheels of the railway industry, the bottom dog, leaves his post, a substitute **must** be found for him immediately. **This then, gives us the value of a General Manager,** and his usefulness to the Company from which he draws such an enormous salary.

And now, au revoir, we shall meet again on the battlefield in the near future, and we shall remember your tactics in the past.

THE PADDINGTON RAILWAYMEN

Appendix Four

What it cost the GWR

	1926	*1925*	*Difference*
	£	£	£
Gross Receipts	29,914,515	35,242,137	-5,327,622
Expenditure	26,814,052	29,457,722	-2,643,670
Dividend (year)	3%	7%	
Deficit after payment Dividends*	2,253,001	930,893	+1,322,108
Pass Train Rcpts	12,529,901	13,833,900	-1,303,999
Goods Trn Rcpts	13,795,969	16,852,730	-3,056,761
of which			
Coal, Coke etc.	3,891,272	6,205,733	-2,314,461
	(26.8m tons)	*(49.5m tons)*	*(-22.7m tons)*
	Million Miles	*Million Miles*	*Million Miles*
Miles run by Company's engines	79.2	94.7	-15.5

What the Chairman said at the AGM (23rd February, 1927)

. . . most disappointing accounts submitted to you within living memory . . . We carried 21 million fewer passengers . . . We have saved upwards of 15 million engine miles, but [this] has been offset . . . by the increased cost and poorer quality of the foreign coal we were forced to buy . . . The actual additional cost of the coal consumed in 1926 amounted to £714,000.

The cost to the country has been estimated at £500,000,000.

* made good from reserves

Appendix Five

Statistics

Statement Shewing Number of Volunteers Enrolled at the Central Volunteer Office, Paddington

Section	Number Enrolled	Number Utilised					Number Not Utilised				
		From Outside Company's Service	*Company's Servants*	*Retired Company's Servants*	*Women*	*Total*	*From Outside Company's Service*	*Company's Servants*	*Retired Company's Servants*	*Women*	*Total*
Traffic:											
General	3,193	769	267	8	32	1,076	1,560	230	59	268	2,117
Signalmen	252	169	62	-	-	231	21	-	-	-	21
Shunters	126	75	4	-	-	79	32	15	-	-	47
Guards	77	17	36	-	-	53	6	18	-	-	24
Lampmen	27	6	10	-	-	16	-	11	-	-	11
Goods:	514	114	159	2	-	275	183	20	29	7	239
Road Transport:											
Motor	379	108	29	-	2	139	220	14	1	5	240
Horse	233	93	11	-	4	108	106	4	-	15	125
Locomotive	694	198	14	23	-	235	441	10	8	-	459
Engineering and Electrical	125	22	-	-	-	22	89	12	2	-	103
Total	5,620	1,571	592	33	38	2,234	2,658	334	99	295	3,386

Statement Shewing Number of Volunteers Enrolled at the Centres Other than Paddington

Division	Number Enrolled	Number Utilised				Number Not Utilised			
		From Outside Service	*Company's Servants*	*Retired Company's Servants*	*Total*	*From Outside Service*	*Company's Servants*	*Retired Company's Servants*	*Total*
Bristol	2,981	970	616	67	1,653	839	432	57	1,328
Exeter	625	135	34	44	213	372	-	40	412
Plymouth	818	133	-	19	152	642	-	24	666
Gloucester	425	71	25	16	112	241	39	33	313
Newport	139	84	2	10	96	34	-	10	43
Cardiff	553	150	42	17	209	296	8	40	344
Swansea	1,495	719	15	8	742	659	67	27	753
Worcester	1,212	213	261	32	506	389	284	33	706
Birmingham	2,029	525	260	29	814	815	347	53	1,215
Chester	517	117	30	5	152	184	153	28	365
Oswestry	155	36	36	7	79	66	-	10	76
	10,949	3,153	1,321	254	4,728	4,536	1,330	355	6,221

Statement of Number of staff on Strike Daily

Grade	*No. of Staff*	*May 5th*	*May 6th*	*May 7th*	*May 8th*	*May 9th*	*May 10th*	*May 11th*	*May 12th*	*May 13th*	*May 14th*
Clerical and Technical Staff	11,998	3,258	3,204	3,166	3,162	3,164	3,122	3,080	3,042	2,969	2,946
Supervisory Staff, including Station Masters and Agents	4,156	871	852	846	857	857	849	852	846	826	813
Engine Drivers	6,202	6,123	6,117	6,115	6,110	6,107	6,105	6,101	6,098	6,050	6,052
Firemen	6,241	6,212	6,215	6,209	6,210	6,210	6,200	6,187	6,187	6,147	6,145
Guards	4,145	3,997	3,999	3,996	3,998	3,986	3,990	3,976	3,957	3,919	3,906
Signalmen	4,843	4,459	4,471	4,393	4,379	4,377	4,334	4,301	4,259	4,083	4,029
Shunters	2,810	2,742	2,684	2,725	2,729	2,735	2,738	2,735	2,726	2,707	2,695
All other Conciliation Grades	38,839	35,993	35,771	35,721	35,794	35,682	35,530	35,410	35,234	34,084	34,256
Shopmen	27,426	25,493	25,332	25,472	25,517	25,516	25,577	25,534	25,478	25,327	25,386
Power Station Staff	260	173	209	203	207	208	210	210	209	198	209
Other Grades	4,559	1,522	1,525	1,529	1,515	1,503	1,516	1,491	1,486	1,488	1,418
Total	111,475	90,843	90,379	90,375	90,468	90,345	90,171	89,877	89,522	87,798	87,855
Dock Staff	4,866	4,288	4,363	4,356	4,432	4,439	4,424	4,424	4,414	4,409	4,401
Grand Total	116,341	95,131	94,742	94,731	94,900	94,784	94,595	94,301	93,936	92,207	92,256

Statement Shewing the Percentage of staff on Strike Daily

Grade	*No. of Staff*	*May 5th*	*May 6th*	*May 7th*	*May 8th*	*May 9th*	*May 10th*	*May 11th*	*May 12th*	*May 13th*	*May 14th*
		%	%	%	%	%	%	%	%	%	%
Clerical and Technical Staff	11,998	27.2	26.7	26.4	26.4	26.4	26.0	25.7	25.4	24.7	24.6
Supervisory Staff, including Station Masters and Agents	4,156	21.0	20.5	20.4	20.6	20.6	20.4	20.5	20.4	19.9	19.6
Engine Drivers	6,202	98.7	98.6	98.6	98.5	98.5	98.4	98.4	98.3	97.5	97.6
Firemen	6,241	99.5	99.6	99.5	99.5	99.5	99.3	99.1	99.1	98.5	98.5
Guards	4,145	96.4	96.5	96.4	96.2	96.2	96.3	95.9	95.6	94.5	94.2
Signalmen	4,843	92.1	92.3	90.7	90.4	90.4	89.5	88.8	87.9	84.3	83.2
Shunters	2,810	97.6	95.5	97.0	97.1	97.3	97.4	97.3	97.0	96.3	95.9
All other Conciliation Grades	38,839	92.7	92.1	92.0	92.2	91.9	91.5	91.2	90.7	87.8	88.2
Shopmen	27,426	93.0	92.4	92.9	93.0	93.0	93.3	93.1	92.9	92.3	92.6
Power Station Staff	260	66.5	80.4	78.1	79.6	80.0	80.8	80.8	80.4	76.2	80.4
Other Grades	4,559	33.4	33.5	33.5	33.2	33.0	33.3	32.7	32.6	32.6	31.1
Total	111,475	81.5	81.1	81.1	81.2	81.0	80.9	80.6	80.3	78.8	78.8
Dock Staff	4,866	88.1	89.7	89.5	91.1	91.2	90.9	90.9	90.7	90.6	90.4
Grand Total	116,341	81.8	81.4	81.4	81.6	81.5	81.3	81.1	80.8	79.3	79.3

Statement Shewing the Number of Staff on Strike in the Principal Departments

Department	No. of Staff	May 5th	May 6th	May 7th	May 8th	May 9th	May 10th	May 11th	May 12th	May 13th	May 14th
Traffic	27,501	21,404	21,141	21,063	21,001	20,983	20,844	20,682	20,517	20,067	19,870
Goods	13,717	9,704	9,710	9,706	9,722	9,723	9,788	9,847	9,826	9,758	9,734
Docks	4,866	4,288	4,363	4,356	4,432	4,439	4,424	4,424	4,414	4,409	4,401
Locomotive	45,666	42,340	42,086	42,164	42,296	42,192	42,230	42,156	42,075	41,816	41,882
Engineering	16,398	13,771	13,799	13,760	13,756	13,756	13,645	13,547	13,478	12,623	12,850
Signal	2,491	2,050	2,046	2,068	2,086	2,083	2,055	2,043	2,029	1,960	1,938
Other Departments	5,702	1,574	1,597	1,614	1,607	1,608	1,609	1,602	1,597	1,574	1,581
Grand Total	116,341	95,131	94,742	94,731	94,900	94,784	94,595	94,301	93,936	92,207	92,256

Statement Shewing the Percentage of Staff on Strike in the Principal Departments

Department	No. of Staff	May 5th	May 6th	May 7th	May 8th	May 9th	May 10th	May 11th	May 12th	May 13th	May 14th
		%	%	%	%	%	%	%	%	%	%
Traffic	27,501	77.8	76.9	76.6	76.4	76.3	75.8	75.2	74.6	73.0	72.3
Goods	13,717	70.7	70.8	70.8	70.9	70.9	71.4	71.8	71.6	71.1	71.0
Docks	4,866	88.1	89.7	89.5	91.1	91.2	90.9	90.9	90.7	90.6	90.4
Locomotive	45,666	92.7	92.2	92.3	92.6	92.4	92.5	92.3	92.1	91.6	91.7
Engineering	16,398	84.0	84.2	83.9	83.9	83.9	83.2	82.6	82.2	77.0	78.4
Signal	2,491	82.3	82.1	83.0	83.7	83.6	82.5	82.0	81.5	78.7	77.8
Other Departments	5,702	27.6	28.0	28.3	28.2	28.2	28.2	28.1	28.0	27.6	27.7

TRAINING OF VOLUNTEER DRIVERS AND FIREMEN

Division	*VOLUNTEERS TRAINED*		*VOLUNTEERS EMPLOYED*	
	Drivers	*Firemen*	*Drivers*	*Firemen*
Bristol	46	116	46	89
Cardiff	15	27	15	27
Old Oak Common	89	130	66	106
Neath	30	45	30	34
Newport	34	54	34	54
Newton Abbot	22	51	20	39
Oswestry	19	36	18	32
Wolverhampton	44	61	39	52
Worcester	23	44	20	39
Totals	322	564	288	472

VOLUNTEERS TRAINED:	
Drivers	322
Firemen	564
	886

VOLUNTEERS EMPLOYED:	
Drivers	288
Firemen	472
	760

Acknowledgements

Ian Coulson of BR
Fred Cole
Mr J. Harber
Richard Morris
John Allen
Philip Kelley and the Great Western Trust
Ken Endersby
John Laver
Nevill Bridger ('Railwayana' bookdealer who kindly lent documents for copying)
Chris Turner
John Worthy of Brunel University (which looks after the Clinker Collection)
Gerald Jacobs
Ralph Tutton
Mr J. Cobley, Editor of the *TSS Journal* (the newspaper of the TSSA)
Don Steggles of the Railway Studies Library, Newton Abbot
Ken Smith
John Gillham for the two maps.
Messrs Weidenfeld & Nicolson for permission to quote from *The General Strike* by G.A. Phillips
Messrs Forge Books and David Watts (grandson of Sir Felix Pole) for permission to quote from *Felix Pole, His Book*
Messrs Lawrence & Wishart for permission to quote from *The General Strike of 1926* by John Murray and *The General Strike 1926* by Jeffrey Skelley

Bibliography and Sources

The General Strike May 1926 published by the GWR (1926)
The General Strike of 1926 by J. Murray (Lawrence & Wishart, 1951)
The General Strike 1926 by J. Skelley (Lawrence & Wishart, 1976)
The General Strike by J. Symons (Reader's Union, 1959)
Felix Pole, His Book by Felix Pole (Town & Country Press, 1968)
The General Strike 1926: Its Origins and History by R. Page Arnot (Republished 1975 by EP Publishing Ltd)
The General Strike by G.A. Phillips (Weidenfeld & Nicolson, 1976)
General Strikes and Road Transport by G. Glasgow (Geoffrey Bles, 1926)
Nine Days in May by P. Renshaw (Eyre & Methuen, 1975)
The Railwaymen by P.S. Bagwell (Allen & Unwin, 1963 - history of the NUR)
The Lighted Flame by N. McKillop (Nelson, 1950 - history of ASLEF)
The Railwaymen by R.S. Joby (David & Charles 1984)
The Railway Gazette
The *GWR Magazine*

Various references in the RAIL series at PRO, Kew. These are quoted in the text; they are well scattered at Kew (even when considering only one company) and would benefit from being grouped together.
Material in the Clinker Collection at Brunel University; thanks to Charles Clinker's sense of history many notices etc. have survived.
British Newspaper Library, Colindale.
Some use was made of the NUR Archives at Warwick University but because of the severe restrictions imposed on photocopying there, not as much as I would have liked.

Index

Note: This index does not include reference to locations mentioned in Chapter Six.